P9-DWY-028

EMERGENCY VEHICLE OPERATIONS

ABOUT THE AUTHOR

Tom Barker is the head of the Department of Criminal Justice at Jacksonville State University in Jacksonville, Alabama. A former police officer and a certified police academy instructor, Barker has been conducting research on police corruption and police misconduct for over twenty years. He has written six books and over twenty articles on these topics. In addition, he has conducted numerous workshops and seminars for a variety of police agencies throughout the United States on ethical issues in law enforcement. Barker has served as an expert witness in both federal and state courts on police ethical behavior on numerous occasions.

Barker is a past president of the Academy of Criminal Sciences (1987-1988) and the Southern Criminal Justice Association (1984-1985). He has received numerous awards including the Founders Award from both the Academy of Criminal Justice Sciences and the Southern Criminal Justice Association.

EMERGENCY VEHICLE OPERATIONS

Emergency Calls and Pursuit Driving

By

TOM BARKER, PH.D.

Head, Department of Criminal Justice
Jacksonville State University
Jacksonville, Alabama

CHARLES C THOMAS • PUBLISHER, LTD.
Springfield • Illinois • U.S.A.

Published and Distributed Throughout the World by
CHARLES C THOMAS • PUBLISHER, LTD.
2600 South First Street
Springfield, Illinois 62794-9265

ISBN 0-398-06808-9 (cloth)
ISBN 0-398-06809-7 (paper)
Library of Congress Catalog Card Number: 97-26799

With THOMAS BOOKS *careful attention is given to all details of manufacturing and design. It is the Publisher's desire to present books that are satisfactory as to their physical qualities and artist possibilities and appropriate for their particular use.* THOMAS BOOKS *will be true to those laws of quality that assure a good name and good will.*

Printed in the United States of America
MO-R-3

Barker, Tom.
Emergency vehicle operations: emergency calls and pursuit driving/by Tom Barker.
p. cm.
Includes bibliographical references and index.
ISBN 0-398-06808-9 (cloth). – ISBN 0-398-06809-7 (pbk.)
1. Police pursuit driving. 2. Assistance in emergencies. 3. Tort liability of police.
I. Title.
HV8080.P9B37 1997
363.2'32-dc21

97-26799
CIP

PREFACE

Few law enforcement tasks involve more danger–to officers and third parties–and the likelihood of civil liability than the emergency vehicle operations. Answering emergency calls and engaging in pursuit requires that the officer be adequately trained, properly supervised and directed (and restricted) by policies, procedures and rules. The days of unrestricted emergency vehicle operations, especially high-speed pursuits, by law enforcement officers are over. The public, especially those sitting on juries, and professional law enforcement officers, agencies and organizations will no longer tolerate "macho police cowboys" behind the wheel of a police vehicle.

This book defines law enforcement emergency vehicle operations and examines the liability concerns and provides guidelines for the development of policies, procedures and rules. Pursuit, the most dangerous emergency vehicle operation, is analyzed from the viewpoint that only well-regulated pursuits should be allowed when the danger to the public of the violator remaining at large outweighs the danger to the public created by the pursuit.

The cost benefit analysis for every pursuit is reached by answering three questions that guide every pursuit: when to pursue, what to do during a pursuit, and when to abandon a pursuit. Ultimately, the need for a pursuit and the continuation of a pursuit once it has begun rests with the **Termination Equation**–Justification for the pursuit balanced against the need for immediate apprehension and the risks involved.

CONTENTS

EMERGENCY VEHICLE OPERATIONS

Chapter 1

INTRODUCTION–RODNEY ROOKIE'S FIRST PURSUIT

Officer Ted Brown was instructing his new charge, another spit and polish rookie fresh out of the academy. A usual day of rolling and patrolling. Then it happened. On their way to answer a domestic disturbance call, a 1994 blue T-Bird busted the light in front of Car 35.

"Damn, if I was going five miles faster that jerk would've T-boned us!" Brown said turning in behind the T-Bird.

"We're gonna put that guy in jail," Brown added.

Six-year veteran Brown turned the blue light on, hit the siren, and off he drove. The light blue T-Bird roared into afterburner as the light bar lit up.

"Damn, he's not gonna stop! Oh, no a chase!" Rodney yelled as he nervously tightened his seat belt.

Avenue I was busy. Cars darted across the busy avenue going from one shopping mall to another. The T-Bird wove in and out of the six o'clock traffic heading north on Avenue I at sixty miles per hour. The police vehicle approached seventy in the twenty-five-mile zone as it threaded its way through the heavy traffic in an attempt to catch-up. Rodney had his left hand wrapped in a death lock on the black shotgun barrel that sat in the secure rack between him and Ted Brown. His right hand dug into the seat as they bounced along. Rodney felt he had to relieve himself, but he didn't think Ted would stop so he could go to the bathroom. Someone screamed at Rodney. Who could it be?, Rodney thought. It was Ted.

"Get on the damn radio and tell them we're 10-100," Ted screamed at Rodney.

10-100 meant pursuit. You're supposed to notify dispatch as soon as you go 10-100, Rodney said to himself as he remembered the academy lecture on emergency vehicle operations.

Telephone poles, department stores, fast-food restaurants, service stations, pulled-over cars, cars stopped in the middle of the road, frightened pedestrians holding packages and small children, and water hydrants whizzed by on the right as Rodney tried to remember his lecture on pursuit driving. Oh, Jesus! He's gonna hit somebody. We're gonna hit somebody, Rodney thought as the T-Bird quickly approached Avenue I and 13th. street. The blue flash in front of them ran the red light at Avenue I and 13th street as it turned east. Oh, My God! The light is still red and Brown isn't slowing down, Rodney thought. He started screaming, "Change light, change," as they approached. Cars slammed on their brakes as they saw the police car approach. The light changed. "We're invincible," Rodney screamed as his heart pumped wildly.

Sliding out of their high-speed turn, Ted slapped the mike against Rodney's left arm and shouted. "You work the mike. I told them we're 10-100."

Rodney didn't want to, but he released his grip on the shotgun barrel to pick up the mike wildly bouncing on the seat between them. Rodney held the mike in his left hand, squeezed the seat with his right hand and prayed that he wouldn't wet his pants. The radio kept screaming the same thing, "Car 35, where are you now?" Rodney kept telling them, but they wouldn't stop asking.

The blue flash two car lengths in front of the wide-open police vehicle ran the two way stop sign at Avenue J and 13th street and turned back north on Avenue J. The T-Bird passed two slow-moving vehicles on the two-lane residential road. Car 35 passed the same two vehicles as an oncoming pick-up truck ran up on the sidewalk to avoid the speeding police vehicle. Both cars ran the stop signs at 14th and 15th street.s Residents gathered up playing children. One elderly man shot the police vehicle a middle finger salute. The T-Bird, with the police vehicle now a half a car length behind it turned left at Avenue J and 16th street. "Another red light," screamed Rodney. The fickle "goddess of pursuit" was with them as they ran the light and turned north on the four-lane Avenue I.

Finally, it was over. The T-Bird pulled to the curb four blocks and three stop signs after the turn on Avenue I and 16th street. Ted Brown was out of the police car in a flash. Brown yanked the teenage driver out of the car by the hair and hit him squarely in the nose. Blood spurted from the screaming and crying teenager's face as a horrified Rodney looked on. Within seconds the area filled with officers and police cars. Ted Brown quickly grabbed Rodney by the arm and led him to the back of the police car before the other officers reached them.

"Rodney, that kid hit his nose on the steering wheel when he hit the curb, didn't he?"

"I guess he did if that is what you say, Ted."

A stern looking Ted Brown shot back, "No, that's what you're gonna say, isn't it?"

"Yeah, that's what happened," a perplexed Rodney replied.

The funny looks the other cops gave Rodney made him nervous. Rodney tried to figure out why everyone was looking at him. They were laughing at him, when Sergeant Edwards from roll call approached.

"Rodney go back to Car 12 and have a seat," he said with a sardonic smile.

Sergeant Edwards talked to Ted Brown for 15 minutes as Rodney sat in the car. Every few seconds cops came by pointed at him and laughed. Rodney couldn't figure out what was wrong. Finally, the sergeant got in the car and turned toward the Interstate.

"Rodney, we're going to Central Headquarters. I want you to hear something."

During the eight-mile drive, the two were silent. Arriving at Central Headquarters, Rodney followed the sergeant down several corridors until they came to a door marked Communications. A balding lieutenant let them in. When they were in the room, a smiling lady sitting behind a console spoke.

"Sergeant Edwards, is that the rookie who was operating the radio?"

"Yep, that's him," was the reply.

Sergeant Edwards, the lieutenant and Rodney moved over to what looked like a giant reel to reel stereo player. The lieutenant took one of the tapes off, moved to another tape player and started rewinding it. Now and then, he hit the play button. Radio transmissions and responses were heard.

"This is Car 35. We're 10-100 North on Avenue I," an excited voice erupted from the tape.

Rodney recognized the voice. It was Ted Brown. A female voice asked.

"Car 35 what's your location now?"

Rodney recognized the next voice even though it was loud and more of a scream than a response.

"We're right behind them."

The room erupted into laughter at the next exchange.

"Car 35, where exactly are you?"

"We're right behind them. We're right behind them. Real close behind them," the excited voice kept repeating.

Could this or has this happened in your police department? Could you, or have you reacted like Rodney during a chase? Have you met Ted Brown or Rodney? If the scenario described above happened in your department would it violate written policies and procedures? Does your department have written policies and procedures covering police pursuits? What, if anything, did Officer Ted Brown do wrong during the pursuit? If there had been an accident with injuries or deaths could Officer Brown convince a jury that his actions were reasonable and prudent under the circumstances? Should the officers have initiated the pursuit? What should they have done differently, if anything, during the pursuit? Should the pursuit have been abandoned? When? What would you do differently or the same as Officer Brown did? Answer these questions now and see if your answers change after reading this book.

Chapter 2

DEFINITIONS

Mission of the Police

> **AS A LAW ENFORCEMENT OFFICER**, my fundamental duty is to serve mankind; to safeguard lives and property; to protect the innocent against deception, the weak against oppression or intimidation, and the peaceful against violation or disorder, and to respect the Constitutional rights of all men to liberty, equality and justice. **LAW ENFORCEMENT CODE OF ETHICS**

However lofty and ideal this first paragraph of the **Law Enforcement Code of Ethics** may be, it is the standard by which we judge the behavior of all law enforcement officers and their respective agencies. According to Webster, duty refers to obligatory tasks, conduct, service, or functions that arise from one's position (as in life or in a group). Those who take the oath of office as law enforcement officers accept as duties the behaviors outlined in the **Law Enforcement Code of Ethics.**

What, if anything, does this have to do with police emergency vehicle operations? A great deal. For starters, any discussion of police behavior or operations must have as its starting point the duties outlined above. And, as Louis Mayo, a former National Institute of Justice official and well known expert on police pursuit stated in *Law Enforcement News*:

> If you say that a fundamental mission of the police is to protect life, then for a police officer to take a nonthreatening situation and escalate it to a life threatening situation is in direct contravention of their mission to protect life (May 31, 1989:13).

Is it possible that law enforcement officers take nonthreatening situations and escalate them into life threatening situations during emergency vehicle operations? Yes, they often do? How? Why do they do it? Can we lessen the possibility of this happening? Yes. How? I intend to answer these questions. However, we should define some terms before we get too far ahead of ourselves.

Authorized Emergency Vehicles

What are emergency vehicles? The definition varies by state and statute. However, most states use the definition contained in the Uniform Vehicle Code proposed by the National Committee on Uniform Traffic Laws and Ordinances:

> ***1-104-Authorized emergency vehicle**–Such fire department vehicles, police vehicles and ambulances as are publicly owned, and such other publicly or privately owned vehicles as are designated by the commissioner (or other appropriate state official) under *15-111 of this act. (National Committee on Uniform Traffic Laws and Ordinances, 1987:1)

Other vehicles may be designated as such, but there is universal agreement that publicly-owned fire and police department vehicles and ambulances are authorized emergency vehicles. In addition to providing a definition of emergency vehicles, the Uniform Vehicle Code provides a special status for emergency vehicles and exempts them under certain circumstances from some traffic regulations.

11-106-Authorized emergency vehicles

a. The driver of an authorized emergency vehicle, when responding to an emergency call or when in the pursuit of an actual or suspected violator of the law or when responding to but not upon returning from a fire alarm, may exercise the privileges set forth in this section, but subject to the conditions herein stated.

b. The driver of an authorized emergency vehicle may:

1. Park or stand, irrespective of the provisions of this chapter;
2. Proceed past a red or stop signal or stop sign, but only after slowing down as may be necessary for safe operation;
3. Exceed the maximum speed limits so long as he does not endanger life or property;
4. Disregard regulations governing direction of movement or turning in specified directions.

c. The exemptions herein granted to an authorized emergency vehicle shall apply only when such vehicle is making use of an audible signal meeting the requirements of 12-401 (d) and visual signals meeting the requirements of 12-214 of this act, except that an authorized emergency vehicle operated as a police vehicle need not be equipped with or display a special visual signal from in front of the vehicle.

d. The foregoing provisions shall not relieve the driver of an authorized emergency vehicle from the duty to drive with due regard for the safety of all persons, nor shall such provisions protect the driver from the consequences of his reckless disregard for the safety of others.

The overwhelming majority of the states have incorporated the Code into their statutes without change. Some have modified it with slight changes. One recent change to the Georgia Statute should be noted.

State of Georgia-40-6-6. Authorized emergency vehicles.

d. 1. The foregoing provisions shall not relieve the driver of an authorized emergency vehicle from the duty to drive with due regard for the safety of all persons.

2. When a law enforcement officer in a law enforcement vehicle is pursuing a fleeing suspect in another vehicle and the fleeing suspect damages any property or injures or kills any person during the pursuit, *the law enforcement officer's pursuit shall not be the proximate cause or a contributing proximate cause of the damage, injury, or death caused by the fleeing suspect unless the law enforcement officer acted with reckless disregard for proper law enforcement procedures in the officer's decision to initiate or continue the pursuit. Where such reckless disregard exists, the pursuit may be found to constitute a proximate cause of the damage, injury, or death caused by the fleeing suspect, but the existence of such reckless disregard shall not in and of itself establish causation.*

3. The provisions of this subsection shall apply only to issues of causation and duty and shall not affect the existence or absence of immunity which shall be determined as otherwise provided by law. (Italics supplied)

Police liability for third party injuries caused by the fleeing suspect, as mentioned in section 2 above, will be examined later.

Limitations on Emergency Vehicle Operations

It is important to understand that state statutes limit or restrict the exemptions granted to emergency vehicles. There must be an emergency, or as the prevailing case law indicates the officer must **reasonably** believe there is an emergency, or a pursuit situation. Otherwise, the police vehicle must obey all rules of the road. As the Uniform Code outlines, under emergency or pursuit circumstances a police officer may park or stand without restriction. Obviously, the parking or standing without restriction applies to accidents, fires, or other emergencies when police officers are controlling the movement of traffic and pedestrians. Emergency vehicles may proceed past a red light or stop signal or sign, but only after slowing down for safe operation. Intersections are the most frequent accident locations for police emergency vehicles. Often, because the emergency vehicle did not slow down to ensure safe passage. This in many cases leads to a *prima facie* (legally sufficient to establish a case unless disproved) case that the emergency vehicle did not slow down for safe operation. An authorized emergency vehicle may exceed maximum (posted) speed limits so long as they do not endanger life or property. Furthermore, an emergency vehicle can disregard traffic regulations governing direction of movement or turning.

The final restriction placed on the operation of emergency vehicles by most state statutes is that the police driver must be making use of his\her emergency equipment (lights and siren) and driving with **due regard** for the safety of all persons. Due regard for the safety of others, particularly in civil actions, is determined by (1) the method by which the officer/s determined the real or apparent emergency, (2) the officer's driving behavior during the emergency or pursuit, and (3) the reason for continuing or not terminating the pursuit. Generally, the police behaviors which determine if the due care principle was violated are: excessive speed, not using emergency equipment, disobedience of traffic signals (lights or signs), passing in no passing zones, going wrong way on one-ways, driving conditions at the time or the reason (initiating offense) for the pursuit.

Emergency–Emergency Call

There is no commonly agreed upon legal definition of what constitutes an emergency or an emergency call. However, case law generally defines an emergency as a situation in which there is a high probability of death or serious injury to an individual (violent crime in progress, accident with injuries), or serious property loss (fire, natural disaster). The IACP has defined an emergency call as:

> An emergency call is a request for immediate police assistance needed to save a life or to prevent a victim from sustaining further serious injury (Training Key 113).

The Mobile, Alabama Police Department offers a unique perspective on the definition of an emergency from the officer's point of view.

What are emergencies from a police officer's point of view?

a. Officer in need of assistance.
b. Hold-up in progress,
c. Scene-to-hospital transportation,
d. Person has swallowed poison; is burned; is in shock; is afflicted with uncontrolled arterial bleeding; has multiple injuries,
e. An area wide emergency status has been (sic) declared

Source:Mobile Police Academy-May 1988-Handout #PGO 34A p.3.

They also provide criteria for judging whether or not a situation is a true emergency.

Criteria for Judging Whether or Not a Situation Is a True Emergency

If it is a true emergency the answers to the following questions will be yes:

a. Is there a possibility that this situation could cause death or injury to an individual?
b. Is there significant property imperilled?
c. Is there anything that I can do to lessen the severity of this situation?

Once all these questions have been answered in the affirmative you are free to act in the due regard of others. (Source: Ibid, p.6.)

However, when one defines emergency there is consensus that the situation is determined by the danger involved, the need for immediate action, and the ability of the responding officers to do something about it. There is also consensus that the emergency response is guided by the principle of due regard for the safety of others. The driving behavior of the officers should not aggravate the emergency situation and make it more dangerous.

The officer in any emergency driving situation (pursuit or emergency call) must drive in a defensive driving posture and never assume what the actions of other drivers will be. He or she must:

1. Never assume that emergency equipment has actually made other drivers aware of their presence.
2. Never approach any intersection at a speed faster than would permit a safe stop should a hazard suddenly appear.
3. Always be prepared for the unexpected, "stupid," driving maneuver on the part of others in the traffic environment.

4. Never assume that they have the right-of-way regardless of the intersection being approached (Auten, 1989:210).

How Dangerous Is Emergency Response?

The use of official statistics reported by police agencies on emergency vehicles operations (emergency calls and pursuit) are continuously criticized for underreporting the number of incidents and the injuries and deaths attributed to them. Nevertheless, the 1994 statistics on persons killed in crashes involving emergency vehicles by the National Highway Traffic Safety Administration, Center of Statistics and Analysis is reported below.

Table 1

Persons Killed in Crashes Involving Emergency Vehicles, by Person Type, Crash Type and Vehicle Type

	Person Type	Single Vehicle	Multi-Vehicle	Emerg.	Emerg.	Emerg.
Police Vehicle Driver	5	2	19	8	24	10
Police Vehicle Passenger	0	0	3	1	3	1
Other Vehicle Occupant	0	0	67	35	67	35
Pedestrian	14	9	1	1	15	10
Other non-motorist	1	0	0	0	1	0

Table 1 does not assign fault, it only reports the number of persons killed. In 1994, there were 24 police vehicle drivers killed and 10 of them were traveling with emergency signals in use. 35 of the 67 occupants of other vehicles killed were killed while the police vehicle was in emergency operation. The table also reveals that 10 pedestrians were killed during emergency runs by the police. After viewing these statistics, a colleague of mine said that 55 deaths was not a high figure given the large number of emergency runs by the police. My response was, "That may be true unless you were one of the fifty-five people or one of their loved ones. Then the number would be high."

NHTSA also reports the number of emergency vehicle and motor vehicle crashes in the years 1988-1994. From 1988 to 1994 there were 1,158 emergency vehicle crashes (police, ambulance, firetruck), 553 (48%) of them during emergency operation. NHTSA also points out that there were 1,317 fatalities in the emergency vehicle crashes 1988-1994; 625 (47%) while the vehicles were operating in emergency use. The statistics do not assign fault and they only report fatalities and not injuries and property losses. However, one can see that emergency vehicle operations is dangerous to all involved: drivers, passengers, occupants of other vehicles and pedestrians.

Myth of the Effectiveness of Rapid Response

Auten (1985) in a well-thought-out examination of emergency driving to crimes in progress attacks, along with others, myself included, the **Popular Police Myth of the Effectiveness of Rapid Response**. He states that two rationales are used to support emergency driving to crimes in progress, (1.) It is necessary to apprehend offenders, and (2.) It is necessary for the protection of innocent bystanders or victims. Statistics from the National Institute of Justice cited in Auten's article says that "response-related arrests occurred in only 3.7 percent of the serious crime calls and 5.6 percent of the less serious crime calls."

The seminal study of police response in the 1977 Kansas City Police Response Study found that the rapid response to 949 calls led to an arrest in only 3.6 percent of the cases. Replication of the study by the Police Executive Research Forum (San Diego, Peoria, Rochester, Jacksonville-Duval County (Florida) also found that arrests attributed to rapid police response were made in only 2.9 percent of the serious crimes. I am not aware of any studies which have confirmed a link between rapid response and on-scene arrests. In fact Bayley (1994:6-7), cites studies that say that "Contrary to what most police think, rapid response is not even a key element in satisfying the public." The public is more interested in predictability rather than rapid response. If the police are called and promise to come, the public wants them to, in fact, come. Bayley says that "It is more important, then, for the police to make reasonable promises they can keep than to reduce average response time by several minutes."

Why is the effectiveness of rapid response a myth? Any five-year veteran street cop could probably answer this question. **Citizen delay in reporting the incident** is the answer. The police have no control over the time taken by victims or witnesses to call. Criminals are long gone by the time a victim or witness gets around to calling the police. Study after study since the 1977 Kansas City study has confirmed this. Auten (1989:196) states that there is a total response continuum.

Total Response Continuum

<u>Time Crime Actually Occurs</u> + <u>Citizen Reporting Delay + Internal Police Department Processing Time</u> + <u>Officer Travel Time</u> = **TOTAL RESPONSE TIME**

Once this total response time exceeds ten minutes, there is no relationship between the police time interval and the probability of a response-related arrest taking place. Bayley (1994) states:

> ....although the police may work heroically to reduce response time, their best efforts will not make a big enough difference to change the outcome. Criminals will almost always have a big head start (p.6)

Police rapid response to major property loss incidents such as fires, explosions, or natural disasters generally has little or nothing to do with preventing these events from occurring or lessening their impact.

Police emergency driving response should be strictly limited to (Auten, 1989):

1. [Serious] Crimes in progress reported with sufficient promptness to demonstrate the strong likelihood of a response-related arrest.

   Emergency dispatchers should be trained to be able to identify these incidents and hold the parties on the line to ensure that there continues to be a strong likelihood of a response-related arrest throughout the emergency response.

2. Incidents involving a direct threat to someone's life or person in which a rapid response by police will diminish that threat.

Even in these incidents excessive speed is seldom warranted. Given the increased risk to the officers and the public, excessive speed to effect a response-related arrest is not warranted when there is approximately a 5-in-100 chance that it will happen.

> Appropriately balancing the inherent dangers of emergency driving with the advantage to be gained by such action is the fundamental point that must be evaluated by an officer in deciding whether to operate his vehicle under emergency conditions. (IACP Training Key #271)

How Dangerous Is Pursuit Driving?

As with emergency response, there are no national statistics collected on pursuit driving. However, the FARS (Fatal Accident Reporting System) system does collect data on fatal accidents involving high speed pursuit. The number of fatalities for the years 1980–1994 are presented in Table 2.

Table 2

Fatalities Involving High-Speed Pursuit Chase with Police in Pursuit by Accident, Year, and Fatality Description.

	FATALITY DESCRIPTION				
	Occupant of Police Vehicle	*Occupant of Chased Vehicle*	*Occupant of Other Vehicle*	*Non-Occupant*	*Total*
Year					
1980	1	244	77	9	331
1981	0	203	56	7	266
1982	0	249	51	7	307
1983	3	229	54	9	295
1984	1	202	36	7	246
1985	5	225	44	5	279
1986	0	242	56	11	309
1987	6	206	39	5	256
1988	0	244	46	6	296
1989	5	223	70	2	300
1990	0	266	46	5	317
1991	4	252	46	5	307
1992	1	224	66	7	298
1993	1	284	57	5	347
1994	3	283	90	12	388
Total	30	3,576	834	102	4,542

Source: FARS 1980-1994

As Table 2 reveals, there were a total of 4,542 deaths reported to FARS in the fifteen-year period 1980-1994. That is an average of three-hundred and three (303) deaths per year. The majority of these fatalities, 3,576 (78%) were occupants of the chased vehicle. However, 834 (18%) of those killed were occupants of other vehicles. Thirty of those deaths were occupants of the police vehicle.

Table 3 provides the breakdown of the 4,542 fatalities by state.

Table 3

Fatalities Involving High-Speed chase with Police in Pursuit by State, Fatality Description-Fars 1980-1994

FATALITY DESCRIPTION

State	*Occupant of Police Vehicle*	*Occupant of Chased Vehicle*	*Occupant of Other Vehicle*	*Non-Occupant*	*Total*
Alabama	2	71	14	6	695
Alaska	0	7	2	0	9
Arizona	1	54	23	0	78
Arkansas	1	27	9	3	40
California	1	582	167	18	768
Colorado	0	43	16	1	58
Connecticut	0	55	8	0	63
Delaware	0	11	0	0	11
Dist. of Columbia	0	5	7	1	13
Florida	1	92	25	4	122
Georgia	1	196	22	2	219
Hawaii	0	7	0	0	7
Idaho	0	19	1	1	20
Illinois	1	168	55	7	231
Indiana	1	77	14	1	93
Iowa	1	43	5	1	50
Kansas	0	23	3	0	26
Kentucky	1	80	10	0	91
Louisiana	1	60	11	3	75
Maine	0	18	5	0	23
Maryland	0	48	8	0	56
Massachusetts	0	86	12	5	103
Michigan	2	131	47	2	182
Minnesota	0	23	2	2	27
Mississippi	0	13	0	0	13
Missouri	0	98	16	3	117
Montana	0	14	2	1	17
Nebraska	0	11	4	1	16
Nevada	0	22	8	0	30
New Hampshire	0	39	4	0	43
New Jersey	0	51	14	9	74
New Mexico	0	24	11	2	37
New York	1	129	33	5	168
North Carolina	1	132	22	5	168

	Occupant of Police Vehicle	*Occupant of Chased Vehicle*	*Occupant of Other Vehicle*	*Non-Occupant*	*Total*
North Dakota	0	9	1	0	10
Ohio	0	119	23	4	146
Oklahoma	5	64	19	0	88
Oregon	0	56	9	0	65
Pennsylvania	2	103	18		126
Rhode Island	0	15	8	1	24
South Carolina	4	55	8	2	69
South Dakota	0	8	0	0	8
Tennessee	2	96	15	5	118
Texas	0	309	101	5	415
Utah	0	11	2	0	13
Vermont	0	28	1	0	29
Virginia	0	69	26	0	95
Washington	0	57	5	2	64
West Virginia	0	36	5	1	42
Wisconsin	1	76	12	1	90
Wyoming	0	8	3	0	11
Total	30	3,576	834	102	4,542

Source: FARS

Table 4 gives the rank order of the top ten states based on the results of Table 3.

Table 4

Ranking of States-Fatalities Resulting from Police Pursuits.
(1984-1994)

Rank	State	Total Fatalities
1	California	768
2	Texas	415
3	Illinois	231
4	Georgia	219
5	Michigan	182
6	North Carolina	168
7	Ohio	146
8	Pennsylvania	126
9	Florida	122
10	Tennessee	118

Source: FARS

Southern states (Texas, Georgia, North Carolina, Florida and Tennessee) are overrepresented in the top ten. There is a need for a closer examination of this and the extremely high figures for

California and Texas. Nevertheless, the conclusion that can be drawn from Tables 3 and 4 is that pursuit driving, like emergency response, is dangerous for all involved, police officers, occupants of the chased vehicle and others using the roadways.

Research Studies

The research studies conducted thus far also indicate that pursuit driving is dangerous. The first examination of police pursuit was conducted in 1968 by the Physicians for Automotive Safety. They concluded that:

1. One out of five pursuits ended in death;
2. Five out of ten pursuits ended in serious injury;
3. Seven out of ten pursuits ended in accidents;
4. One out of 25 killed was a police officer;
5. Four out of five pursuits were for minor offenses; and
6. Police pursuits caused 500 deaths each year.

Their study, although methodologically flawed, did stimulate controversy and calls for additional research. Several of the forthcoming research studies were conducted in agencies with restrictive pursuit policies.

In 1983, the California Highway Patrol (CHP) released their report on 683 pursuits conducted over a six-months period, primarily on freeways. They found that:

1. 198 (29%) of the 683 pursuits resulted in accidents;
2. 99 (11%) resulted in injuries;
3. 7 (1%) resulted in deaths;
4. 27 (4%) were voluntarily terminated by the officer;
5. 429 (63%) of the pursuits were initiated for traffic offenses;
6. 179 (26%) of the pursuits were initiated for serious criminal activity; and
7. 243 (36%) were voluntarily terminated by the driver surrendering.

The CHP study concluded that police pursuits were not as dangerous as had been reported in the media and police textbooks. However, it should be pointed out that the California Highway Patrol operated under a restrictive policy with supervisory control over the pursuits. The Commissioner of the California Highway Patrol, at the time of the CHP study is "convinced that **well-regulated** pursuits are necessary (Hannigan, 1992)." We will return to the idea of **well-regulated** pursuits when we discuss policy issues.

Another research study conducted in departments with restrictive policies cited by Alpert and Dunham (Alpert and Fridell, 1992). The Alpert and Dunham study examined 952 pursuits undertaken by the Metro-Dade Police Department and the City of Miami Police Department in 1985, 1986 and 1987. Among their findings were:

1. 364 of the 952 pursuits (38%) resulted in accidents;
2. 160 pursuits (17%) resulted in injuries;
3. 7 pursuits (.7%) resulted in deaths;
4. 40 pursuits (4%) were voluntarily terminated by the officer;
5. 512 (54%) of the pursuits were initiated for traffic offenses;
6. 19 (2%) of the pursuits were initiated for reckless driving or impaired driving;
7. 312 (33%) of the pursuits were initiated for serious criminal activity.

In 1988, The Minnesota Board of Peace Officer Standards and Training (POST) promulgated pursuit police guidelines for state wide adoption and established a mandatory reporting system for all police pursuits. A year after the policy guidelines and the reporting system was in effect they reported:

1. 823 pursuits were conducted in Minnesota;
2. 358 (44%) of these pursuits resulted in accidents;
3. 194 (24%) resulted in injuries;
4. 2 (.2%) resulted in deaths;
5. 38 (21%) were voluntarily terminated by the officer;
6. 420 (51%) of the violators stopped;
7. 627 (76%) of the pursuits were initiated for traffic offenses;
8. 46 (6%) of the pursuits were initiated for DWI;
9. 133 (16%) were initiated for felonies.

Alpert and Fridell (1992:109) also provide data from a study by Nugent and his colleagues of the Phoenix, Arizona Police

Department 12 months after the implementation of a restrictive pursuit policy.

1. There were 144 pursuits conducted after the policy was implemented;
2. 26 (18%) resulted in accidents;
3. 7 (5%) resulted in injuries;
4. 1 pursuit (.7%) resulted in a death;
5. 60 (42%) were voluntarily terminated by the officer or supervisor.

The overwhelming conclusion from the small number of research studies that we have on police pursuit is that there is a need for national pursuit statistics. However, there are some conclusions that can be drawn from the data that we have thus far on police pursuit.

Research Conclusions

Based on the studies cited and others I have reviewed, I have arrived at the following conclusions:

1. Emergency vehicle operations, particularly high-speed pursuit, is probably the most dangerous of all police activities.

2. There are more police vehicle chases each year than police shootings.

3. The police kill and injure more people each year during police chases than they do with their firearms.

4. The highest percentage of accidents occurring during pursuits are reported in small agencies and the lowest percentage are reported in very large agencies.

5. Pursuits at any speed and for any length of time are dangerous, approximately 30-40% involve traffic accidents.

6. A significant number of the accidents that occur during pursuits result in injuries and deaths and many of the victims are

innocent civilians not connected to the pursuits.

7. The overwhelming number of pursuits are initiated for minor traffic violations.

8. The fleeing driver is seldom a fleeing felon.

9. The majority of pursuits are initiated between 2000-0400 hours.

10. Pursuits are most likely to occur on Friday, Saturday, or Sunday.

11. The majority of pursuits are of relatively short duration, i.e. 10 minutes or less. However, it should be understood that 10 minutes or less at speeds in excess of 80 miles per hour covers a large distance.

12. The majority of injuries and deaths can be reduced by the adoption and implementation of a sound emergency operation policy.

The overwhelming deduction from the limited research is that emergency driving, especially high-speed pursuits, should be engaged in only as a last resort and the apprehension of the fleeing violator should never be the sole factor to be considered in a pursuit. Furthermore, the rapid response to an emergency call is not the sole factor to be considered when responding to an emergency situation.

Urboyna (1991) states that there are three aspects of police pursuits, [I would add all police emergency vehicle operations] that make it apparent that all pursuits should be scrutinized.

> 1. The potential harm present during pursuit–all pursuits are dangerous.
>
> 2. The reason that police officers generally pursue–traffic offenses.
>
> Even though some traffic offenses, such as speeding, may at first appear to warrant police intervention to stop the danger presented to others, police intervention can increase rather than lessen the danger.
>
> 3. The availability of other means either to apprehend individuals or to stop the need for pursuits.

In addition to more research on this topic, each agency should keep an accurate record of each pursuit that occurs. The problems associated with pursuit and answering emergency calls are local problems. The agency should have a post-pursuit form to be filled out after **every** pursuit. The absence of an accident should not be considered to be a successful pursuit. Luck could have been responsible. At a minimum, this post-pursuit form should ask for time, day, primary unit, assisting units, the initiating offense. General information such as traffic conditions, roadway and weather conditions should be recorded. Obviously, any injuries, deaths or property damage must be described.

The problems associated with pursuits can only be solved locally through effective written directives: policies, procedures and rules, and training. Therefore, accurate data collection on each and every emergency vehicle operation must be maintained. Many agencies are already doing this. Unfortunately, the majority are not. Most law enforcement agencies do not begin the policy development process or training until after they have been forced to by a serious accident, involving death or injury, or by court following a civil suit. Change is coming. Forced or willing. Change is coming. **The Days of Unrestricted High-Speed Pursuit, Especially for Traffic Violations, Are Over.**

Chapter 3

LIABILITY CONCERNS

America is a litigious society. We have more lawyers than any civilized country in the world. I was once told that suing each other is the second most favorite indoor activity in this country. That may be an exaggeration. However, there is no doubt that Americans are quick to say, I'm going to sue, whenever they feel they have been wronged. There is also no denying that lawsuits against law enforcement officers and agencies have risen dramatically in recent years.

Lawsuits arising from police pursuits are just behind those involving use of force. As I often tell police academy students: If you are engaged in a pursuit or emergency response where there is an injury or death, the chances are above 75 percent that you are going to be sued. The typical lawsuit lists the officer/s involved, the shift supervisor, the chief and the city as the plaintiff goes after the deep pocket. I also tell these same students that what we teach them can not lessen the chance that they will be sued, instead we attempt to lessen the possibility of a successful suit. Lawsuits, or the possibility of lawsuits, are an occupational hazard of American law enforcement.

This book is written for a larger audience than my Alabama academy students. Therefore, most of what follows is in general terms. Specific state statutes and case law will have to be consulted to determine the liability of individual officers and departments in the various states.

Law enforcement officers, as we have seen, are permitted by statute to engage in emergency vehicle operations. They are also granted certain exemptions from the traffic laws governing other drivers. However, these same statutes restrict the actions of the emergency vehicle driver, e.g., use of emergency equipment, due regard for the lives and property of others using the highways, etc. Police officers have a statutory duty to drive with due regard for the safety of others. The citizens who are injured, killed–in this case their estates, or damaged during emergency vehicle operations can seek redress through the judicial system at either the state or federal level. Whenever a civil suit is filed against a law enforcement officer or agency, this redress is predicated on two basic legal concepts:

1. That police officials were negligent in performing their various duties and responsibilities.
2. That the actions by police officials were in violation of some particular statutory, civil or constitutional right of an individual (Traffic Institute, 1982:1).

and is known as **civil liability**–the legal obligation of a person to compensate a person whom he/she has injured. The basic concept of civil liability is that persons are only liable for injuries they have caused by behavior considered to be a departure from ordinary, prudent behavior.

There are three categories of torts (private wrongs, other than breach of contract) under which civil liability is based.

Three Categories of Torts

1. **Negligence**–Unintentional torts caused by a departure from the duty to exercise due care.

Remember, I said earlier that the duty to exercise due care was incorporated in the Uniform Traffic Code and state statutes. A defendant is liable if he/she could have or should have anticipated that his/her actions would result in injury to another.

2. **Intentional Torts**–In this case the defendant deliberately intends to injure another person, his property or his/her protected rights. Examples are assault and battery, wrongful death, false arrest and imprisonment, malicious prosecution and, in the pursuit situation, forcible stop techniques.
3. **Constitutional Torts**–The defendant officer or agency has failed to recognize and uphold the constitutional rights, privileges, and immunities of others.

Recall that the first paragraph of the **Law Enforcement Code of Ethics** stated: (law enforcement officers were to) "respect the Constitutional rights of all men to liberty, equality and justice."

Civil Liability–State Laws

Liability under state law generally arises from negligent torts, and can be against persons or property. The officer's mental state is important in distinguishing between negligence and intentional torts. In negligent torts the officer's mental state is irrelevant or unimportant. Negligent torts most often arise from omission (failure to act) rather than commission (intentional acts). To prove an act was intentional the injured party must show that the officer/s made a conscious decision to commit an act which was excessive under the circumstances (use of deadly force to effect a misdemeanor arrest) or engaged in behavior which posed an extreme danger to the public (busting through a red light without stopping or pursuing without emergency equipment in use). The officer intends or should have expected the results.

The judge or jury in determining negligence will apply the "reasonable man's standard" in determining liability. In other words-Would a reasonable person of ordinary prudence in the position of the defendant have behaved the way the defendant did? Factors, to be discussed later, such as speed through intersections, road and weather conditions and the need for emergency response will be considered in determining reasonableness. Would a reasonable man have conducted the pursuit in the same manner as described in Chapter 1?

In order for liability to attach, the plaintiff must prove the following elements:

1. A duty on the part of the officer or department to act with due care toward the plaintiff–injured party.

The prevailing emergency vehicle state statutes are introduced to establish the duty of due care. The officer has a legal duty to drive his vehicle in a manner that does not create an unnecessary risk to others. This is usually incorporated into departmental policy. In fact, any citizen traveling the highways has to act with due care for others using the roadways. Law enforcement officers have a higher duty to do so.

2. While carrying out this duty, the officer breached or violated the standard of care established for a police officer under the same or similar conditions.

Did the officers actions create an unreasonable risk to others? At this point established or commonly accepted standards for emergency vehicle operations will be examined.

3. The plaintiff must show that there was an injury or damage to the plaintiff.
4. Lastly, the plaintiff must show by the preponderance of evidence (the standard of proof in a civil action is preponderance of evidence not beyond a reasonable doubt) that the officer's actions are the proximate cause of the injury or damage.

There must be a close or causal link between the officer's negligence and the injury to the plaintiff.

In order to determine the officer's liability, individual state laws and court cases must be examined because the general definitions given above are modified and superseded by law and court cases in different jurisdictions. Negligence is determined on a case-by-case and often varies from one judge or jury to another. According to *Black's Law Dictionary*, negligence is defined as the failure "to do something that a reasonable man would do or something which a reasonable man would not do under the existing circumstances."

Factors Which Determine Negligent Operation of Emergency Vehicles

Rolando delCarmen et al. (1991:159-160) state that the factors that court decisions have determined can be used to demonstrate that there was negligent operation of a police emergency vehicle and can be categorized into four areas:

1. **The justification of the chases**. The courts will look into such matters as (1) whether there existed a real or apparent emergency, (2) whether the offender's conduct was serious enough to justify the chase, (3) whether alternatives to pursuit were available to the officer, and (4) whether apprehension of the suspect was feasible.
2. **The actual physical operation of the vehicle**. The courts will look at such considerations as (1) speed at which the vehicle was operated, (2) the use of emergency equipment, (3) violations of traffic regulations, and (4)disregard of traffic control devices.
3. **The circumstances surrounding the operation**. The courts will look into such items as (1) the physical conditions of the roadway, (2) the weather conditions, (3) the density of traffic, (4) the presence of pedestrians, (5) the presence of audio or visual warning devices, and (6) the area of pursuit.

4. **Departmental considerations.** The courts will look into such concerns as (1) whether there was a violation of departmental policy regarding police pursuits, (2) whether the officer had been trained in pursuit driving, and (3) the physical and visual condition of the police vehicle.

Schofield (1988) is even more explicit in his list of factors that determine the extent of pursuit liability.

Eight Factors Which Determine the Extent of Pursuit Liability

1. *Purpose of Pursuit*
   What is the need or reason for the pursuit? Does the reason warrant the risks involved? Has the violator only committed a traffic violation? Could the violator be apprehended at a later time?
2. *Driving Conditions*
   This involves a general assessment of equipment, weather, roadway and traffic conditions.
3. *Use of Warning Devices*
   Warning devices, emergency equipment, is a statutory requirement in most states during emergency vehicle operation. Nevertheless, the overreliance on warning devices which leads to reckless actions can create a liability risk.
4. *Excessive Speed*
   Speed, especially speed when crossing an intersection against the light or a sign, is a critical consideration.
5. *Disobeying Traffic Laws*
6. *Roadblocks*
   Did the roadblock place innocent persons in jeopardy? Was it authorized by a supervisor? Was the roadblock placed in a highly visible area that gave motorists and the violator ample time to stop?
7. *Use of Force*
   Force such as firearms, ramming, boxing, bumping or spike strips should be used only when authorized by a supervisor and only when authorized by law and departmental policy. Whether or not the officers have been trained in their use will also become a liability issue.

8. *Continuation of the Pursuit*
   A pursuit that is continued when the level of danger of the pursuit outweighs the benefits to be gained will increase the level of liability. Would a reasonably trained police officer have continued the pursuit under the circumstances?

Civil Liability-Federal Law Section 1983

Federal civil liability of law enforcement officers and their agencies is based on Title 42 of the United States Code, Section 1983–Civil Action for Deprivation of Civil Rights.

42 U.S. 1983, Civil Action for Deprivation of Rights

> Every person who, under color of any statute, ordinance, regulation, custom, or usage, of any State or Territory, subjects, or causes to be subjected, any citizen of the United States or other person within the jurisdiction there of to the deprivation of any rights, privileges, or immunities secured by the Constitution and laws, shall be liable to the party injured in an action at law, suit in equity, or other proper proceeding for redress.

There are four basic elements of a Section 1983 Civil Rights Suit.

Basic Elements of a Section 1983 Suit

1. The defendant must be a natural person or a local government.

   The original wording of Section 1983 when it was passed in 1871 applied to only persons, this was modified in 1978. In a landmark case the U.S. Supreme Court (1978) in *Monell v. Department of Social Services of the City of New York* held that local government units were "Persons" within the meaning and intent of Section 1983.

2. The defendant must be acting under "color of law."

   The law does not apply to private persons. There must be some misuse of power possessed by a public official by virtue of state law. The deprivation is made possible because the defendant is acting under authority of state law.

3. The violation must be of a constitutional or federally-protected right.

The plaintiff must show that the alleged wrongful action deprived the plaintiff of a right, privilege, or immunity secured by the Constitution or federal law. Most often the claims involve the 4th, 5th and 14th constitutional amendments.

4th–Illegal arrest, illegal search and seizure.
5th–Improper conduct regarding confessions/interrogation.
14th–Violation of due process and equal protection rights.

In the past, there were very few successful federal suits against law enforcement officers and their agencies in the area of emergency vehicle operation. However, three recent U.S. Supreme Court decisions have had a bearing on law enforcement liability during emergency vehicle operations. The first of these was *Tennessee* v. *Garner* (1985). This use of deadly force case set the standard that deadly force may not be used unless the suspect poses a significant threat of death or serious injury to the officer or others. The same year the 5th Federal District Court in *Jamieson By and Through Jamieson* v. *Shaw* (772 F.2d 1205) held that the use of force standard of *Tennessee* v. *Garner* was violated during a pursuit. In this case, a passenger was injured when a fleeing vehicle crashed into a "deadman's" roadblock after the police shined bright lights into the drivers eyes.

Several years later in *Brower* v. *County of Inyo* (1989) the U.S. Supreme Court considered a high-speed chase of over twenty miles that resulted in the death of a fleeing driver of a stolen car. The violator was chased into a roadblock other police officers had created by placing a tractor-trailer across a two-lane road in the middle of the night. There was testimony that the officers had placed a police car in such a manner to blind the driver with the headlights just prior to the roadblock. The court was unanimous in their finding that the driver had been "seized" within the meaning of the Fourth Amendment. According to the court, the officers had executed a "deadman's" roadblock–no avenue of escape or one where the driver does not have time to react. It was an intentional deathtrap. This case signals that other forcible stop techniques such as ramming, blocking etc. may be constitutional violations when the use of deadly force is not justified. That is, the force used does meet the *Tennessee* v. *Garner* standard.

Probably the most significant Supreme Court decision affecting police actions, including emergency vehicle operations is *City of*

Canton v. *Harris* (1989). This decision said that the failure to train can subject the city or municipality to liability if that failure to train amounts to deliberate indifference. Although not concretely defined, the court did provide some guidance on defining deliberate indifference.

> But it may happen that in light of the duties assigned to specific officers or employees, the need for more or different training is obvious, and the inadequacy so likely to result in the violation of constitutional rights, that the policy makers of the city can reasonably be said to have been deliberately indifferent to the need. (109 S.CT. at 1205)

The now famous footnote 10 elaborated on deliberate indifference.

> For example, city policy makers know to a moral certainty that their police officers will be required to arrest fleeing felons. The city has armed its officers with firearms, in part to allow them to accomplish this task. Thus, the need to train officers in the constitutional limitations on the use of deadly force (see *Tennessee* v. *Garner*, 471 U.S. 1(1985), can be said to "so obvious", that failure to do so could properly be characterized as "deliberate indifference" to constitutional rights. (109 S. Ct. at 1205, fn 10)

Obviously, city policymakers know to a "moral certainty" that their police officers will be required to engage in emergency vehicle operations (emergency response and pursuit). The city has provided vehicles with special equipment on them to accomplish this task. Therefore, it is obvious that the officers must be trained in this area. The Local Government Risk Management Services, Inc., a service organization of the Association of County Commissions of Georgia and the Georgia Municipal Association addressed this issue.

> What does this [Canton] mean to local governments in Georgia? As a minimum, Georgia local governments are going to have to assume that all law enforcement officers are trained and fully understand the proper use of force when facilitating arrests. This assurance must be clearly documented and regular training updates must be made to keep changes and new developments on the forefront of the department's training schedule. This will include such topics as mechanics of arrest, civil rights violations, negligent use of force, deadly force, and negligent use ofmotor vehicles (pursuit and emergency driving) to name a few. In high speed pursuit situations where injury and/or property damage occurs, it is felt that the federal courts may well treat this as the use of force and thus, subject local governments to this opinion. (The Risk Connection. 1(3), May 1989)

Their prediction has come true with the increase of Section 1983 emergency vehicle operation cases. In this same publication, the

Local Government Risk Management Services pointed out the risk of allowing officers to patrol prior to P.O.S.T. training. The safety and liability issues involved in allowing a totally untrained officer to patrol armed and in a police vehicle are staggering. Unfortunately, it still occurs and not just in Alabama and Georgia. I have discussed this issue with many law enforcement executives and their usual response has been–We can't afford to send them to the academy, or there isn't an opening, before putting them on the street. I always respond–You don't have to convince me. Convince the judge or jury because you are going to end up in court. I guarantee that.

Chapter 4

POLICIES, PROCEDURES, RULES AND REGULATIONS

Again, I repeat my caution. There is nothing that I, or anyone else can say or tell an officer and agency that can assure 100 percent liability protection. Police officers and their agencies are sued when they do things "right" and when they do things "wrong." However, when they do things "wrong" they pay the consequences. What I am attempting to do is lessen the possibility of a successful civil action. There are measures that the agency can take to lessen the liability risk. The absence of these measures increases the risk of a successful civil action and, lest we forget, increases the risk of injury and death.

The agency *must*, notice I didn't say should, provide policies, procedures, rules and regulations on emergency vehicle operations–emergency response and pursuit. The statutory law is not, by itself, adequate because it does not provide sufficient direction to the officer/s. The law, statutes, and administrative policies are written for different reasons. That does not mean the applicable legal statutes and court decisions are not taken into account when writing policies, procedures and rules. They are, or better be.

The written directive system with clear and specific policy and its attendant procedures, rules and regulations, is the only way the agency can ensure common understanding and interpretation by all personnel. Policy provides a statement of the agencies objectives and an administrative guide for decision making prior to the act–ground rules for the exercise of discretion. All law enforcement agencies should have policies that address all foreseeable police incidents. Police agencies, no matter their size, must have as a minimum policies that cover all foreseeable high-risk law enforcement critical tasks such as use of force, emergency vehicle operation, etc. In the area of pursuit driving the chief policymaker must balance the conflicting interests of apprehending known offenders against the safety of police officers, fleeing drivers and their passengers and others using the roadways.

I should also add that policy writing is a local agency's responsibility. I have often been asked to write policies for law enforcement agencies. I will provide models, critique developed policies, and assist an agency in writing their policies. However, I steadfastly refuse to write policies for any agency. I do so because the agency's policies reflect the thinking, feelings, local and state laws, and leadership skills of the agency's chief policymaker, not the author. Policy must be tailored to local laws, the community and its various publics, and the political structure. Policy must have the support of the chief administrator. Furthermore, I should point out that the best written policy has no effect if the officers are not trained in it or it is not enforced.

The chief executive officer and his supervisors, in addition to their leadership roles, have specific responsibilities in the area of pursuit policy. At a minimum they should:

1. Establish a written directive system–policies, procedures and rules concerning all aspects of pursuit/emergency vehicle driving.
2. Ensure that the written directive system emphasizes safety first.
3. Distribute, and have it signed, to all personnel who may become involved in a pursuit. They should read and sign in the presence of a supervisor.
4. Ensure that the written directives are discussed with all personnel through the chain of command. This will assure that any possible questions have been addressed.

In addition, the chief administrator must provide mechanically safe police vehicles for his/her officers. He/she should make certain that adequate insurance coverage is available to all personnel in the event of a civil suit.

I should also caution that it is not a good idea to take the policies of another agency and change the name to your agency. This common practice is the lazy persons way out and can get an agency in an embarrassing predicament in court. I often tell the story of a twenty-person police agency that asked me to review their policy manual. I did so and began to notice references to watch commanders and deputy chiefs in the first few pages. I stopped my review and called the chief. I asked him where he got the policies. His reply was that most of them came from LAPD. End of conversation and end of review. What follows is a guide to writing policy.

A Note on Policy Development

Policy is defined as the principles and values which guide the performance of a departmental activity. These principles and values are "attitude forming" in the sense that they tell departmental personnel how to think about performing their duties (Hoy, 1982:301). A policy is *not* a statement of what must be done in a particular situation. It is a statement of guiding principles which should be followed in order to attain some departmental goal or objective. Policy should always be thought of as the framework for drafting procedures and rules and regulations.

Example

IACP MODEL POLICY–VEHICULAR PURSUIT

1. **Purpose**

   The purpose of this policy is to state the guidelines to be followed during vehicular pursuit.

   *It minimizes municipal liability in accidents that occur during pursuit. (NIJ no date).

   Vehicular pursuit of fleeing suspects presents a danger to the lives of the public, officers and suspects involved in the pursuit. It is the policy of this department to protect all person's lives to the extent possible when enforcing the law. In addition, it is the responsibility of the department to assist officers in the safe performance of their duties. To effect these obligations, it shall be the policy of the department to narrowly regulate the manner in which vehicular pursuit is undertaken and performed.

As can be seen by the example above, policy may be very broad and allow some flexibility and it is subject to varying interpretations. Therefore, once it is written the agency must define the terms and limit the flexibility and discretion through procedures, rules and regulations.

Procedures are the methods of performing an operation or the manner in which the task is to be performed. Procedures are different from policy in that they direct the action to be taken within policy guidelines. Policy and procedures are both objective-oriented; however, policy establishes limits of action while procedures direct responses within these limits (Carter & Dearth, 1984). Procedures allow for some flexibility within limits and they are usually found in instructional materials and manuals as well as in policy statements.

Example

IACP MODEL POLICY CONTINUED

III. Definition

A. Vehicular Pursuit: An active attempt by an officer in an authorized emergency vehicle to apprehend fleeing suspects who are attempting to avoid apprehension through evasive action.

*It maintains the basic police mission to enforce the law and protect life and property.

IV. Procedures

A. Initiation of Pursuit

1. The decision to initiate pursuit must be based on the pursuing officer's conclusion that the immediate danger to the public created by the pursuit is less than the immediate or potential danger to the public should the suspect remain at large.
2. Any law enforcement officer in an authorized emergency vehicle may initiate a vehicular pursuit when *ALL* of the following criteria are met:
   a. The suspect exhibits the intention to avoid arrest by using a vehicle to flee apprehension for an alleged felony or misdemeanor that would require a full custody arrest;
   b. The suspect operating the vehicle refuses to stop at the direction of the officer, and
   c. The suspect, if allowed to flee, would present a danger to human life or cause serious injury.

Rules and **Regulations** are actually synonymous and refer to specific requirements or prohibitions which prevent deviations from policies or procedures. A violation of a rule/regulation usually invites disciplinary action. If policies are "attitude forming" and guide judgements, rules are "behavior forming" and govern behavior. They should only be used when absolutely necessary to ensure compliance with some desired behavior or action. Unfortunately, some police administrators often confuse rules with policy and procedures and believe the only way to control behavior is through a proliferation of rules and regulations. This is self-defeating because the proliferation of rules/regulations creates an illusion of control yet not genuine control (Cordner, 1989). This simple solution ignores the purpose of policy development and the effects of training, education and good supervision.

Although too many rules may be counterproductive, there are instances where police behavior or misbehavior must be prevented. In these instances, rules are necessary. Such a case arises with emergency vehicle operations.

Example

IACP MODEL POLICY CONTINUED
RULES/REGULATIONS

F. Pursuit Tactics

1. Unless expressly authorized by a field supervisor, pursuit shall be limited to the assigned primary and backup vehicles. Officers are not otherwise permitted to join the pursuit team, or follow the pursuit on parallel streets.
2. Officers may not intentionally use their vehicle to bump or ram the suspect's vehicle in order to force the vehicle to stop off the road or in a ditch.
3. Departmental policy pertaining to the use of deadly force shall be adhered to during the pursuit.

G. Termination of Pursuit

1. A decision to terminate pursuit may be the most rational means of preserving the lives and property of both the public, and the officers and suspects engaged in pursuit. Pursuit may be terminated by the pursuing officer, the field supervisor or chief executive officer of the department.
2. Pursuits shall be terminated immediately in any of the following circumstances:
   a. Weather or traffic conditions substantially increase the danger of pursuit beyond the worth of apprehending the suspect,
   b. The distance between the pursuit and fleeing vehicles is so great that further pursuit is futile, or
   c. The danger posed by continued pursuit to the public, the officers,

> or the suspect is greater than the value of apprehending the suspect(s).

The National Institute of Justice states that a clearly defined pursuit policy will achieve several ends:

- It gives officers a clear understanding of when and how to conduct a pursuit.
- It helps reduce injury and death.

When writing policy the law enforcement administrator, as a minimum address the following: (1) Mission Statement (protect lives and property); (2) Legal Authorization for Pursuit (the appropriate state statute); (3) Continuation and Termination Factors; (4) Responsibilities of Support Units; (5) Permissible Vehicle Tactics; (6) Interjurisdictional Activities; (7) Review of Pursuit Incidents and (8) Training Requirements. Factors one and two have already been discussed, the remaining factors will be addressed in subsequent chapters. I am thoroughly convinced that most of the safety and liability problems associated with emergency vehicle operations could be eliminated or minimized by effective supervision, a comprehensive, restrictive written pursuit policy, which is constantly refined and strictly enforced.

Two authors, one a chief of police and a past president of the I.A.C.P., who tragically lost a wife and child to a police pursuit, have provided some very practical advice to the law enforcement executive.

> The law enforcement executive who wants to keep his troops under control should ensure that the following tenets are clearly understood.
>
> - You don't always have to get your man.
> - You don't always get your man.
> - A third-party injury involving the public may result in punitive damages–you're on your own.
> - Traffic violators are usually just traffic violators.
> - Emergency runs and pursuits are first cousins–both of them replete with peril to you, the department and the public.
> - The rule is, "primum non nocre" (first do no harm).

- We have entrusted you with a tool (vehicle) for which you have probably had marginal training. Therefore scale down the usage of the tool under stressful conditions. Until top-notch simulators are readily available, you will continue to be marginally trained.
- The media, the courts and the public have high expectations of law enforcement. Let's not undermine their trust or confidence, lest they see us as Jekyll\Hyde drivers.
- The agency head will call for your termination of employment if there is evidence of careless or negative driving, just as he would for careless or negative use of a firearm or baton.
- The "Golden Rule" is in effect. As you would not want your loved ones placed in harm's way, you will not place others' loved ones in needless jeopardy. (Whetsel & Bennett, 1992:30-31)

Several states (e.g. California, Illinois, Maine) have recommended state-wide pursuit policies for law enforcement agencies. There was even a 1992 bill introduced into Congress that would have amended "title I of the Omnibus Control and Safe Street Act of 1968 to increase national awareness concerning high speed motor vehicle pursuits involving law enforcement officers and the individuals pursued..." (H.R. 4429) The National Pursuit Awareness Act of 1992 read in part:

1. accidents occurring as a result of high speed motor vehicle pursuits caused by drug offenders and other motorists fleeing from law enforcement officers are becoming increasingly common across the United States;
2. the extent of this problem makes it essential for all law enforcement agencies to develop and implement both policies and training procedures for dealing with these pursuits;
3. to demonstrate leadership in response to this national problem, all federal law enforcement agencies should develop and coordinate policies and procedures governing pursuits, and provide assistance to state and local law enforcement agencies in instituting such policies and training; and
4. such policies should balance the need for prompt apprehension of dangerous criminals with the threat to the safety of the general public, and should specifically define, at a minimum, what constitutes a pursuit, the requirements necessary to initiate a pursuit, and regulations to continue or terminate a pursuit.

One state, California, has even indemnified police agencies having well-regulated polices.

California Vehicle Code–Pursuit Policy

> A public agency employing peace officers which adopts a written policy on vehicular pursuits complying with subsection (c) is immune from liability...
>
> C. If the public entity has adopted a policy for the safe conduct of vehicular pursuits by peace officers, it shall meet all of the following minimum standards.
>
> 1. It provides that, if available, there be supervisory control of the pursuit.
> 2. It provides procedures for designating the primary pursuit vehicle and for determining the total number of vehicles to be permitted to participate at one time in the pursuit.
> 3. It provides procedures for coordinating operations with other jurisdictions.
> 4. It provides guidelines for determining when the interests of public safety and effective law enforcement justify a vehicular pursuit and when a vehicular pursuit should not be initiated or should be terminated. Cal. Veh.Code. Ch 1205 17004.7 (1987)

C subsection 1 of the California statute points to an often forgotten aspect of pursuit policies–supervisory responsibility and accountability. An agency's pursuit policy–all policies actually–should contain guidelines for those supervisors or senior officers who are responsible for:

1. Determining the number of department units to participate in the pursuit.
2. Coordinating operations with other jurisdictions.
3. Using any available law enforcement aircraft.
4. Determining when the interests of public safety and effective law enforcement justify a pursuit–a vehicle pursuit and when a pursuit should not be initiated or should be terminated; and
5. Evaluating all pursuits and completing a written pursuit report following guidelines established by the agency. (Hannigan, 1992:46)

Safety and liability concerns dictate that all law enforcement agencies take a proactive approach to the writing of restrictive pursuit policies, procedures and rules. Letting the task be forced on them by a serious accident or civil suit is foolhardy and often very expensive.

Chapter 5

PURSUIT

I have been discussing pursuit as if we all understood what I was writing about. That is probably not true. Most assumptions prove false. There are a number of pursuit definitions in the professional and academic literature; however, I rely on two which I believe are simple enough to define the topic in a way understandable to all. A simple definition–Pursuit is the attempt by law enforcement officers to apprehend a suspect(s) in a motor vehicle while that suspect(s) is trying to avoid apprehension. Another good definition taken from the Broward County (Florida) Sheriff's Office is: Vehicle Pursuit occurs when a suspected violator clearly exhibits the intention of avoiding arrest [or citation] by refusing to stop and using a vehicle to flee. Both definitions assume the following facts–the law enforcement officer is in an authorized emergency vehicle, the suspected violator is aware of the attempt to stop him/her [on rare occasions the driver may not be aware because of alcohol, drugs or mental illness] and is resisting that attempt, and the violation can be a traffic offense, misdemeanor or felony.

The law enforcement officer(s) has two obligations during any pursuit:

1. The police have an obligation to apprehend a violator, and to prevent them from doing any harm to others using the highways. However, they have a greater obligation to,
2. Not make things worse and conduct the pursuit in a manner that is not careless, reckless or wanton.

Duty to drive with "due care" during emergency operations is, as I said earlier, specifically dictated in all state statutes. The police duty to avoid damage or injury to innocent third parties is superior to that of pursuit or emergency response (U.S. Department of Justice, NHTSA). Law enforcement officers must understand that as this nation's cities and highways become more congested, pursuits (especially for routine traffic violations) become increasingly hazardous and dangerous. The manner in which an officer responds to an emergency call and initiates and conducts a pursuit can mean the difference between property damage, injury and even death.

The limited number of possible outcomes of a pursuit (see below) dictate that pursuits are to be avoided whenever possible and conducted with restraint when they cannot be avoided.

Four Possible Outcomes of a Pursuit

1. The suspect pulls over and is apprehended.
2. The suspect loses the pursuing officer.
3. The pursuit becomes so dangerous that the officer terminates it.
4. There is an accident.

If neither party (officer or violator) terminates the pursuit (voluntarily or involuntarily, i.e., runs out of gas, mechanical breakdown, etc.) there are only two possible outcomes–escape or crash.

Schultz has said that there are six typical drivers who may attempt to elude (1979:4):

1. Juvenile drivers who do not have a driver's license and have "borrowed" a parent's or relative's car.
2. Juveniles who have stolen a vehicle and, knowing it to be crime (joyriding), are willing to attempt a "run" to avoid capture.
3. A driver with a bad driving record who realizes that "just one more" citation will suspend his or her driver'slicense.
4. A driver with a record of driving while intoxicated who has been drinking and fears a license suspension.
5. A driver who has committed a prior minor crime fears major consequences if caught.
6. A driver with contraband in the vehicle–narcotics, stolengoods, burglary tools, illegal firearms, etc,–fearing a major arrest for a minor traffic stop.

As can be seen by the six categories of drivers outlined above, the typical violator that flees is not a dangerous felon. Study after study has confirmed this finding. Officer after officer has used this excuse. If they run, they could be a felon–to justify a dangerous pursuit.

There is a tendency by some to reduce all complex problems to simple solutions. This has occurred in the discussion concerning pursuit. Some have reduced the argument to two extreme positions–

pursue all or pursue none. Proponents of high-speed pursuit, whatever the consequences, feel it is necessary to prevent potentially dangerous criminals from eluding the criminal justice system and committing more crimes. Therefore, they would support a policy of pursue all those who run. They would argue that restricting pursuits would violate the law enforcement officers duty to protect the public and enforce the law.

I have also heard the ridiculous argument that if the public knew that police officers would not pursue them no one would stop–everyone would run. As we saw earlier, the typical event which initiates a pursuit is a traffic violation. The overwhelming majority of traffic citations are issued to normally law-abiding citizens who would not "run" from the police under any circumstances. Even, the overwhelming majority of DUI's will stop when signaled to pull over. A no-pursuit policy would not result in everyone "running" from the police whenever they were signaled to pull over.

On the other hand, a no-pursuit under any circumstances is also a mistake. There are limited times when pursuits are necessary. There are criminals who have committed major crimes who will attempt to avoid capture at any costs. They would be a threat to the public and law enforcement officers if they were allowed to escape arrest. There are also instances when a violator has had too much liquor or drugs and his/her driving creates an extremely hazardous condition for those using the roadway. Persons with mental problems may also drive in a hazardous manner that must be stopped before they injure or kill themselves or others. Fortunately, the person/s in these categories are rare and represent only a small percent of all the pursuits that take place. However, even the pursuits of these violators must take place in a manner that does not increase the risk for the public.

The ultimate question that remains to be answered is if we cannot rule out all pursuits and we cannot allow pursuits for all violators–When should pursuits be conducted? **Well-regulated** pursuits should be allowed when the danger to the public of the violator remaining at large outweighs the danger to the public created by the pursuit. Only safe pursuits should be allowed. This costs benefits analysis is reached by answering three questions: when to pursue, what to do during a pursuit, and when to abandon a pursuit.

Chapter 6

FIRST QUESTION–WHEN TO PURSUE?

Discretionary Decision

The patrol officer is generally the first decision-maker in answering the question–when to pursue. Nevertheless, the decision to pursue should be a difficult one for the law enforcement officer and it should be a guided decision. It is not automatic–when the suspect runs, chase him. It is a decision guided by caution, sound judgment, policies, procedures, rules/regulations and training. The officer must refrain from overreacting and take the required few seconds necessary to make a safe and rational judgment. The officer must not let peer pressure enter into his/her decision.

The officer's attitude at this decision point is very important. Decision-making must be based on a low-risk, high-gain attitude. He/she must realize that the police vehicle is a deadly weapon and that they are more likely to be involved in an accident than a shooting. Overconfidence in driving abilities, impatience, pride, and feeling "ticked off" often lead to tragedy.

It is well-known that some officers use their vehicles "as outlets for their 'macho' instincts or as tools to alleviate boredom, anxiety or hostility" (Whetsel & Bennett, 1992:30). Police "cowboys" who love to chase and even bait suspected violators into running are well-known in many departments. They must be kept under control. Otherwise, they will push themselves too hard and past the point when the pursuit should have been terminated. Always remember that the public has a right to expect that their law enforcement officers are the protectors of their lives and property. In addition, they have the right to assume that their police will comply with the traffic laws, act as a positive example to the community and have been trained in how to react to sudden emergency situations.

Stages of Pursuit

According to Auten (1985) most pursuits go through five stages. We will discuss the first three stages in this chapter and the remaining stages later.

STAGE 1–The Relaxed Stage

The violation occurs or the suspect is spotted. Routine. The officer signals the violator to pull over. He or she turns on the blue/red light and, maybe even, taps the siren. There is no indication that the violator is not going to stop. The officer assumes that this will be another routine traffic stop.

STAGE 2–The Alert Stage

The violator or the suspect disregards the signals to pull over and starts to increase speed or take other evasive action. The officer senses trouble. The officer's adrenal glands start producing adrenaline. Pulse and heart begin to pump faster and his/her vision focuses tightly on the violators vehicle. Speed increases speed as the officer narrows the gap between him/her and the violator. The siren is activated. The officer reaches for the mike to begin radio communication. The Oh S___, thoughts form in the officer's brain. The need for rational, not emotional, decision-making increases.

STAGE 3–The Controlled Stage

The officer catches up to the violator. He/she is communicating to dispatch. The officer has not gone 10-100 yet, but it won't be long. The police driver's focus of vision is totally on the suspect and his/her emotions are still somewhat under control. The majority of all potential pursuits end here as the violator or suspect pulls over. An irritated police officer calls the tag number in for a wants and warrants check. A tight-jawed officer approaches the violator/suspect with citation book in hand.

For those who do not pull over and increase their speed or evasive action the officer must decide if pursuit is warranted. Do I pursue?

As I said in the last chapter, the issue is not whether or not the police should ever pursue. Under some circumstances they should. However, we are interested in the conditions and manner to conduct pursuits in the safest possible manner. **Only safe pursuits should be allowed.**

There are a number of limiting factors that determine the answer to the question–when to pursue?–and whether or not the pursuit will be safe.

Known Initiating Offense

The nature and seriousness of the **known initiating offense** is the first limiting factor. The law and accepted police standards and practices do not require that the officer has some sort of psychic powers or a crystal ball. However, it is expected that the officer makes his/her decision of what they know and not what they speculate. Obviously, the misdemeanor vs. felony distinction is an important consideration is deciding whether to begin a pursuit and how long to continue it. Nevertheless, it should never be assumed that those that "run" must be guilty of some felony. We have seen that the research conducted does not support this assumption. Law enforcement officers know this, in spite of what they say publicly. The"they run because they have committed some other offense, probably a felony"myth is perpetuated by the police because it is a useful justification and a C.Y.A. technique. The most common pursuit-initiating offense is a traffic violation. Is and always has been.

Traffic Violations

a. *Nonhazardous violations*

Violations such as equipment (no taillights, one headlight, loud mufflers, etc.), registration (no tag, expired tag, etc.) or completed violations (e.g. passing a red light or stop sign) seldom, if ever, warrant pursuit, especially high-speed pursuit. A traffic stop should be attempted, but generally the conditions are not right for a pursuit. If there is an accident, the officer will always have to deal with the possibility that the violator did not create a hazard until the pursuit began and would have ceased to be a hazard if the pursuit was terminated.

Why might a person who has committed a nonhazardous violation run? (see Chapter 6). A pursuit can create more hazards than the original violation because of "psychological force" created during the pursuit. To my knowledge, Urbonya (1991), was the first to use this specific term in describing police pursuits. However, she states that police experts [She cites D.P. Blaricom and Geoffrey Alpert.] agree with her. She says that there are two types of force that can occur during a pursuit. Physical force occurs when a police vehicle collides with an individual's vehicle. It can also occur through the use of other forcible stop techniques.

Psychological force occurs as a result of the pursuit and often compels the violator to continue his flight until he crashes or the officer abandons the pursuit. Alpert [telephone conversation cited in Urbonya] states that the speed of the officers may control the speed of the violator who is fleeing. Furthermore, once police officers decide to pursue there is no reason for the individual to stop. There are, in most states, no increased criminal or traffic violations for the individual because they have already committed the offense. In those states that have increased the penalties for eluding the police, there is even less incentive to stop. Escape may appear the best way to avoid the increased penalties.

b. *Hazardous Violations*

Hazardous violations are those which present a continuing danger to other road users. They **sometimes** require immediate and aggressive pursuit. Driving under the influence of alcohol or drugs (which will not be known until the violator is stopped or wrecks) reckless driving, or driving at excessive speeds are examples of hazardous traffic violations. Although the officer pursues what he/she believes to be a hazardous violator, they are not relieved of the duty to drive with "due regard" for the safety of all persons nor are they protected from the consequences of any reckless disregard for safety.

Roadway and Traffic Conditions

Roadway and traffic conditions at the time of the initiating violation are limiting factors to be considered. During periods of congestion, such as morning or evening traffic, pursuit may be impossible or extremely hazardous. Every officer is, or should be, familiar with roads on his/her patrol area that are extremely dangerous. They may be hilly, full of downgrades, marked by intersections or access roads (strip malls, convenience stores, driveways, etc.) or have curves that obstruct vision. Or perhaps, the roads are narrow and without adequate shoulder room to allow third parties to safely get out of the way. This creates a situation where one or more vehicles; the violator, civilian drivers, or even pursuing vehicles may be forced into the oncoming lanes of traffic with disastrous results.

Another roadway condition considered in the decision of when to pursue is the condition and the type of road surface (asphalt, gravel, under construction, etc.). The irregular shape, size, and weight of gravel stones on an uneven surface can cause them to move about easily. This can cause a vehicle to go out of control with slight movements. Braking on gravel can cause a vehicle, especially at high-speeds, to slide. A police vehicle following the pursued vehicle will also be pelted with flying stones. This obscures vision. Blacktop surfaces will bleed oil to the surface during hot, humid days resulting in a slick surface. The presence of rain, especially a light rain which can bring up the oil from the roadway and make it extremely slippery. Concrete surfaces can have dips in them as the earth settles under them. There is also the possibility of potholes on concrete surfaces.

Weather conditions such as snow, ice, sleet, rain, wind and fog alter visibility, braking and acceleration. Many of these conditions can obscure the edge of the road, lane markings, and traffic signs. Rain is an extremely hazardous driving condition. As little as 1/16th of an inch could cause hydoplaning which affects steering and braking. Rain also distorts images.

Weather conditions also affect the siren's audibility. The siren may be heard sooner on an overcast or cloudy day. On clear days the siren tends to dissipate into the atmosphere. Fog also affects the siren's distance audibility. The greater the distance the greater the sound blockage.

The presence of intersections, driveways, business exits, malls along the pursuit path must be considered. Drivers, not aware of the pursuit, not hearing the siren, and not seeing the emergency lights may suddenly and unexpectedly obstruct the roadway. Obviously, the presence of fog, haze, smoke and mist will affect visibility.

Traffic density will create unique problems in rural and urban areas that may mitigate against pursuits. In rural areas, the officer must be alert for livestock, pets, school buses, children waiting for buses, and slow-moving vehicles such as tractors, farm implements, and trucks. Urban areas will have traffic entering from alleys, parking lots, driveways, children playing in the streets, delivery vehicles, drivers exiting parked vehicles, pedestrians, school crossings and crosswalks.

The officer's familiarity with the roadway being traveled, or about to be traveled if he/she decides to pursue must be considered. To pursue a violator, especially at high speeds, on unfamiliar roadways compounds the hazards to the officer, the violator and others using the roadways.

Police Vehicle Type and Condition

Unmarked police vehicles not equipped with siren or emergency lights will never engage in pursuits. The emergency vehicle statutes of all but four states specifically state that emergency lights and sirens are required for emergency operation. Nevertheless, every year there are lawsuits arising from accidents involving police pursuits conducted by law enforcement vehicles not equipped with emergency equipment. Some of these lawsuits involve traffic violations. The author is aware of one wrongful death lawsuit where three plainclothes narcotics officers in a unmarked pickup truck engaged in a traffic violation pursuit. Such actions do not pass the common sense test.

Unmarked law enforcement vehicles equipped with a siren and an emergency light that can be affixed to the dash or the top of the vehicle should not become involved in pursuits, especially for traffic violations, except in extreme circumstances. If involved in a pursuit, they should discontinue pursuit when assistance can be obtained by a marked vehicle with a siren and more visible emergency equipment. It is too hazardous for unmarked police vehicles to engage in pursuits. There is always the danger of a violator, or suspected violator, not knowing that the pursuing vehicle is in effect a police vehicle. There have been numerous examples of this happening.

Three-wheel motorcycles will not engage in pursuit of traffic violators under any circumstances. Two-wheel motorcycles should engage in pursuits only under extreme circumstances and then only for short periods of time. As soon as assistance can be obtained from a marked police vehicle–automobile–they should discontinue pursuit.

Every motor vehicle has a maximum safe speed at which it can be operated. Some of the other vehicle limiting factors are:

a. brake conditions–worn, glazed, hot;

b. suspension–heavy duty, responsiveness;

c. emergency vehicle warning devices;

d. known mechanical failures–steering, coolant, etc.;

e. tires–worn, underinflated etc.

The principle mechanical danger in a prolonged high-speed pursuit is the strength of the tires. Speeds over 85 miles an hour require special tires warranted by the manufacturer. I often tell the students in the police academy to consider that the vehicle they are driving at high speed and the tires on it may have been "bought at the lowest bid." A scary thought, indeed.

An officer should get in the habit of making a safe vehicle inspection prior to each tour of duty. This inspection should include a mechanical inspection (looking under the hood for proper fluid levels; worn belts and hoses; loose wires; and any other loose, worn or broken items), an interior inspection (brakes and emergency brake, horn, P.A. system and siren, gauges and warning devices, fuel, safety belts, mirrors, and door locks) and an exterior inspection (tires, air pressure and tread; mirrors, windows, lights; headlights, taillights, emergency lights, spotlights; and damage to the vehicle. This inspection is done for safety reasons and to assign responsibility for damage.

Time of Day and Geographic Location

The time of day, including the visibility associated with it (daylight, dusk, darkness), is a limiting factor in the decision of when to pursue. Engaging in pursuits when other motorists and pedestrians are most likely to be using the roadways, e.g. from 7:00-8:00 AM and 4:00-6:00 PM on weekdays is extremely dangerous and seldom worth the risk it creates, especially for traffic offenses, misdemeanor or nonviolent felonies. The potential dangers they create to others usually outweighs the results to be gained from a successful apprehension. When measured against the reasonable man's standard–would a reasonable man have pursued under the circumstances–they come up short. Any reasonable man, especially a trained police officer, should realize that pursuing a violator in rush hour traffic to write a traffic citation or make a misdemeanor arrest is too dangerous and not worth the risk it creates.

Night driving presents problems that makes pursuit, especially high-speed pursuit, risky. Night driving reduces visibility and hides potential hazards. It is more difficult to judge the speed and position of another vehicle at night. Glare from roadside lighting and the headlights of other vehicles can impair the officer's vision.

The geographic location of the initial violation and possible routes the pursuit may follow (e.g. school, residential, business, urban, rural) is a factor to consider in any pursuit decision. The officer must always keep in mind where the pursuit is now and where it is heading.

Human Factors

Anyone who has ever been involved in a pursuit, especially a high-speed pursuit, can attest to the high level of stress endured by the officer. This stress can, and often does, affect the officer's risk-taking decisions. The officer's attitudes and emotions become significant factors in deciding whether or not to pursue, often, to the exclusion of all other factors. The "police machismo" image leads to numerous pursuits that are too dangerous from the beginning. And, unfortunately, the decision to pursue is easier than the decision to terminate. Therefore, many pursuits that were too dangerous from the start are not terminated when they should be. Officers often engage in and continue pursuits because they fear that fellow officers will think they are cowards or timid.

Once involved in a pursuit the officer may fall victim to "pursuit fixation." That is he/she becomes so engrossed in the apprehension of the violator that the safety of others is forgotten or ignored. The officer's only thoughts are "get that jerk." The longer pursuits continue, the more likely that pursuit fixation will occur.

Physical factors such as fatigue, drugs, shift work, and medical conditions affect a driver's ability to act and react in pursuit situations. They should be taken into account in the initiating decision by the officer and his/her supervisor. The senses such as vision, hearing, smell and touch all provide input data for pursuit decision-making. Known deficiencies in these areas must also be considered.

Vision is particularly important because it supplies 90-95 percent of incoming data. At high speeds peripheral vision narrows, depth perception is less accurate, vision distorts, and color or night vision capability is reduced.

Availability of Assistance

Traffic violator pursuits, especially of a long duration, are extremely hazardous when assistance is not available or when assisting units must drive long distances to provide aid. It is not uncommon for officers working the midnight shift in the region served by the police academy I lecture in to be the only police officer in the county or within 25-50 miles. It is foolhardy to pursue under such conditions.

Possibility of Alternative Actions

Pursuit, especially prolonged high-speed pursuit, is a last resort option. Whenever safer alternative actions are possible they should be taken. Well-known examples of alternative action are: securing an arrest warrant when the violator is known or providing enough information as possible to the dispatcher for an arrest at a later time when the identity of the violator becomes known. Information provided to the dispatcher can also lead to a traffic stop made by another officer under safer conditions.

Nonpolice Passengers

Units that have prisoners, witnesses, suspects, complainants, or other nonpolice passengers will *never* become involved in pursuit situations. The nonpolice passengers mentioned above are supposed to be protected, not endangered, by their contact with the police. This is especially true for prisoners.

A special case of nonpolice passengers are interns and ride-alongs. We face this situation all the time. Our criminal justice student interns ride with police officers on a daily basis. They all sign liability waivers before being assigned to the agency. However, in this state it is not possible to waive negligence liability. Therefore, if the student is injured or killed during a pursuit and it can be shown that the injury or death was the result of the officer's or agency's negligence they are liable. As a general rule, we have the agency agree that our student interns will not be involved in pursuits. Any law enforcement agency should consult legal counsel before allowing interns or ride-alongs to ride in police vehicles.

The decision to pursue, as we have seen, is not an automatic response. The limiting factors must be taking into consideration. They must be specifically mentioned in the agency's policies, procedures and rules. And, they must be reinforced through the agency's training programs. A well-directed and well-trained officer is the key to ensuring that only safe pursuits are initiated.

Chapter 7

SECOND QUESTION–WHAT TO DO, OR NOT DO, DURING THE PURSUIT?

The officer, after considering all the limiting factors has now decided that it is safe to pursue. What should he or she do next? We are now in what Auten calls the fourth stage of the pursuit.

STAGE 4-The Anxiety Stage

This stage begins when the officer realizes that the fleeing vehicle really isn't going to stop. Now, the officer's emotions really heighten, adrenalin dump occurs, and vision sharply focuses on the fleeing vehicle. Often, basic driving habits are ignored. The officer begins to worry that he/she might lose the fleeing violator. The untrained driver may lose reason and common sense at this point. He/she is **10-100, in pursuit.**

The officer should immediately activate the emergency lights and siren and notify the dispatcher. Many law enforcement agencies require permission from a supervisor at this point. No permission–no pursuit. The Charleston, South Carolina Police Department is one of these agencies. They took the decision-making process out of the hands of the pursuing officer and gave it to the street supervisor. At first, officers reported that they couldn't hear the supervisor's response because of vehicle, road and radio noises. This was solved when the department instituted a "no response is a terminate" policy (Whetsell, **LEN**).

Communication

Communication skills at this point are crucial. Officers must accurately and precisely use the radio. The radio is the pursuing officer's only source of communication with the dispatcher and fellow officers. It increases the likelihood of help if needed. The radio is the officer's best weapon if used properly. The dirt bags don't have the ability to call for assistance. Yet. The tone of the voice should be calm, natural and relaxed. Emotions must be kept under control, although this will be a hard task. Remember Rodney from the first chapter. First, tell the dispatcher who you are. If you have a partner, there should be a prearranged plan about who will work the radio in an emergency. Transmit the following information to the dispatcher:

a. The exact violation justifying the pursuit.

b. Location, direction, approximate speed of the car being pursued and road name and conditions.

c. Detailed description of the vehicle; make, model, year, color, number of doors, and distinguishing marks or characteristics, and license plate.

d. Identification of the fleeing driver and occupants; number of occupants, occupant descriptions.

Occupant information is extremely important. Often, occupants are unwilling participants in the pursuit. They may even be trying to persuade the driver to stop. In these cases, the driver is needlessly putting them at risk of injury and death, the officer should not increase that risk by engaging in an unsafe pursuit–more on this later.

e. Request assisting officers and a supervisory opinion.

Headlights

During daylight hours, headlights should be used with emergency lights. The use of wig-wag headlights is especially useful. Headlights are often more discernible than the traditional red or blue overhead lights during the daytime. Most drivers will see the headlights before they hear the siren or see the overheads. For those of you who are skeptics, have one of your buddies come up a mile behind you, turn their headlights, emergency lights and siren on. Which of the lights do you see first? Which are the easiest to see? Do you hear the siren? **NO**. Even the car's emergency flashers are useful during the daytime. That is, if they do not interfere with the functioning of the brake lights and turn indicators.

At night, it is best not to use the high-beam headlights. They often obliterate the emergency lights and blind oncoming traffic.

Emergency Equipment

When Using Emergency Equipment Remember the Following Rules:

RULE NUMBER 1. Emergency Lights and Siren Do Not Make You Invincible.

Unfortunately, some officers fall victim, literally and figuratively, to the **Invincibility Syndrome** when they turn on their emergency equipment. This is a false sense of security. There is no force field around the speeding police vehicle when the lights and siren are activated.

RULE NUMBER 2. The Use of the Emergency Equipment Is a Request for the Right of Way. The Emergency Equipment Does Not Grant the Right of Way Nor Does the Law Allow You to Take It.

The emergency equipment, lights and siren are there as warning devices. They warn the public that an emergency vehicle is approaching and is supposed to allow them to yield the right of way. We cannot have emergency vehicles running over and into citizens who do not or cannot (crowded conditions, fear, etc.) yield the right of way. Approaching and passing slower vehicles with your emergency equipment on is extremely dangerous. Never assume that they will pull to the right and let you pass safely. Unfortunately, they are as likely to stop, speed up, turn left, run off the road, etc. Make sure you know what they are going to do before passing. I have seen, viewed videos, and examined civil and criminal cases where officers with their emergency equipment engaged have passed slower moving vehicles on the right. If there is an accident when the vehicle pulls to the right on the approach of an emergency vehicle and is struck by that emergency vehicle, the only defense I can think of is utter stupidity. The responsibility for safe driving always rests with the officer.

Speed

The officer in a pursuit of a violator should maximize control over his/her vehicle by adjusting the speed of his/her vehicle to traffic, road, and weather conditions. State statutes do not grant law enforcement officers any **legal right** to drive at excessive speeds. However, law enforcement officers, by statute, have a legal and moral obligation not to endanger the lives, health, or property of others using the roadways.

According to IADLEST (International Association of Law Enforcement Directors of Law Enforcement Standards and Training, 1986), collision data indicates that driving too fast for conditions occur most often in approaching: intersections, hills, curves, and passing slower traffic.

Speed is especially critical at intersections. The officer, according to statue, must slow down to ensure safe operation. Therefore, the officers should:

1. Adjust their speed to allow for other drivers to adjust to the police vehicle's approach.
2. Adjust their speed to allow others to see and hear the emergency warning devices.
3. Visually search the intersection–left, front, and right.
4. Look for additional emergency response vehicles.

   This includes, ambulance, fire, rescue, and law enforcement vehicles. Many collisions have occurred between emergency vehicles at intersections during pursuits and emergency operation.

5. Change siren pattern to attract attention with a different sound.

The officer should understand that as speed increases, the effectiveness of the siren decreases. Other drivers and pedestrians may not have sufficient time to react to the sound of the siren. At high speeds overtaken drivers may not hear the siren until the police vehicle is one or two car lengths behind the vehicle. Most third party injuries occur because the third party had no warning prior to the accident. They didn't hear the siren, they didn't see the lights or they didn't have time to react. Oftentimes, the third party will not know what to do or how to do it. They haven't read what to do since they took their driver's license examination.

Caravaning

I have seen the following descriptors used when discussing **Caravaning** during pursuits: ridiculous, wasteful, dangerous, hazardous, ludicrous, Keystone Cops, infectious, unjustifiable, and asinine. I agree with all of them. What possible law enforcement purpose can be served by 5, 10, 15, 20, 25 police vehicles all in a row chasing one violator? I can't think of one. The only objective such behavior accomplishes is to greatly increase the likelihood of an accident. It also provides comic relief for those watching the nightly news on TV.

Why do police vehicles line up one behind the other at high speeds and chase the same vehicle? They do so because no one is in charge of the pursuit and every one wants to get in on the act. Contrary to popular belief, police work is generally boring and filled with repetitive tasks. Therefore, when something happens officers want to get in on the action. Caravaning is a clear indication that emotions and not reason are guiding the pursuit.

Following such spectacles on the news, I have been asked if the caravaning police cars could communicate with one another during the pursuit. I usually reply, probably not. Then the question becomes why did they do it? I just shrug my shoulders and move on. What can I say?

During pursuits, there should be two, possibly three, police vehicles actively involved in the pursuit. The first vehicle will be the primary unit–the unit that initiated the pursuit, a unit following the primary unit–a secondary unit, and possibly a third unit–the supervisory monitoring the pursuit. Other units should monitor the pursuit and not become actively involved unless assigned by a supervisor. Supervisors can assign supporting units to run parallel streets, cut off cross traffic, and get into position if it is necessary to use some forcible stop technique. However, additional units should not become actively involved unless assigned. Limiting the number of police vehicles reduces the possibility of collisions between police vehicles converging into a single area and reduces the danger of police/citizen accidents.

Use of Force

Forcible Stop Techniques

Forcible stop techniques such as roadblocks (stationary and rolling), ramming, bumping, and channelization are to be used as last resort options and then under limited, safe circumstances. Research findings have concluded that:

1. The use of forcible stop techniques results in high suspect capture rates. However,
2. Their use is likely to result in traffic collisions with deaths and injuries.

Before considering the use of forcible stop techniques the supervisor should (I do not believe that pursuing officers should make the decision to use forcible stop techniques. A cooler head not involved in the pursuit, a supervisor, should make this decision.) base his/her decision on: (1) Whether or not the use of deadly-forcible stop techniques are the application of deadly force-is legally and morally justified in the situation and; (2) Whether the existing conditions will permit forcible stop techniques to be used without increasing the hazard level to the public (Auten, 1988).

Additional factors to be considered prior to using forcible stop techniques are:

1. The condition of the road surface.
2. The number of available traffic lanes.
3. The volume of traffic present.
4. The speed of other vehicles.
5. The possible reaction of other drivers to the pursuit.
6. The availability of other police units.
7. Escape routes available to the fleeing suspect.
8. Geographic locale.

Auten (1988) also cautions that before attempting a forcible stop technique the officer must:

1. Make certain via communication that other units know that a forcible stop technique is going to take place, what that technique will be and where it will take place.
2. If the technique requires more than one police vehicle, the officer must ensure that the assisting vehicles are in position.
3. Divert civilian traffic away from the location.

Furthermore, Auten (1988) states that forcible stop techniques have two goals, to induce the suspect to stop and to actually force the suspect to stop. Induced techniques do not involve actual contact between the officer and the suspect. He considers the use of spikes to be a combination of induced and forced techniques.

Forced/Induced Forcible Stop Techniques

Stationary Roadblock–Induce to Stop

Placing an object-motor vehicle, barricade, portable stop signs, or other physical devices on the roadway to impede or alter the normal flow of traffic. The roadway is not completely blocked. Should be used in isolated areas with no visual obstruction. A straight, level, road with, if possible, no intersecting streets or other escape routes should be chosen.

Stationary Roadblock–Forced to Stop

These roadblocks (deadman's)-present the suspect with two options: stop or crash. There are no escape routes. They are only used in deadly force situations. Arresting the driver of a stolen car is not, I repeat is not, a deadly force situation.

Rolling Roadblock–Induce to Stop

These roadblocks involve causing the suspect to gradually slow to a stop. They require two or three police vehicles surrounding the vehicle. To be properly executed, they require training, precision driving, communication and coordination. Not to be attempted at high speeds or by unmarked police vehicles.

Ramming–Force to Stop

This the most dangerous of all forcible stop techniques and must be used only in the most extreme circumstances. Ramming can result in the loss of control of one or both vehicles. A vehicle out of control is a deadly weapon. If possible, it should only be used when the suspect will be forced off the right side of the road onto a soft, obstruction-free surface, i.e., a vacant field.

Channelization–Induce to Stop

This technique is used to force the suspect into a path selected by the officer, e.g., dead end, into a roadblock or where spikes have been set up. The officers must block all possible routes except the one selected by the officers.

Caution–The high speeds and congestion possible on most highways makes the actual blocking (partially or totally) an extreme danger to innocent occupants of motor vehicles. Therefore, they should only be used when the safety of the public is absolutely assured and when they are essential to the apprehension of dangerous persons. A more commonly used and safer approach is the use of (at the side of the highway) lights and signs, a police vehicle/s or other devices, directing vehicles to reduce speed and to pull off the road (Maine, Law Enforcement Manual). These are attempts to convince the violator of the futility of further efforts to escape.

Firearms

From a legal standpoint, the officer may only be justified (I said justified, not has the right) in firing at or from a moving vehicle during a pursuit *only* to defend him/herself from an armed attack, other than the use of the vehicle, which the officer believes could result in death or serious bodily injury. However, it must be understood that firing at or from a moving vehicle is an extremely dangerous maneuver that is seldom worth the risk. The U.S. Department of Justice as early as 1987 has advised against such actions.

Shooting, at or from Moving Vehicles

Officers should not discharge a firearm at or from a moving vehicle except as the ultimate defense of another when the suspect is using deadly force by means other than the vehicle.

RATIONALE:

1. Difficulty in hitting the target.
2. Ricochets striking innocent persons.
3. Population densities.
4. Difficulty in penetrating the automobile body and steel belted radial tire.
5. Inability to put a stop to vehicle momentum even when the target suspect is hit. [If the suspect is hit, the vehicle will become an extremely dangerous unguided missile.]
6. Assuming the responsibility for damage or injury which might result from causing the vehicle to go out of control.
7. Difficulty in hitting a moving target.

The International Association of Chiefs of Police in their 1989 Model Pursuit Policy reiterated this warning concerning shots at or from moving vehicles.

Shots at or From Moving Vehicles (IACP)

> The Model Policy also prohibits shots at or from moving vehicles. Such shots are, as in the foregoing situation (warning shots), considered an unacceptable risk to innocent bystanders. It should also be recognized that most conventional police handguns are typically ineffective in readily disabling or stopping a motor vehicle. Such firearms, in fact, will normally not penetrate auto bodies, steel-belted automobile tires that are in motion, and frequently breach auto safety glass.
>
> While line officers are prohibited from firing at or from a moving vehicle, there are circumstances in which trained tactical officer may take such actions if deemed appropriate by command personnel. Even under these circumstances, such actions should be taken only when all reasonable alternatives have been exhausted, when a failure to take such action would probably result in death or serious bodily harm, and when due consideration has been given to the safety of innocent bystanders.

We must face the inevitable question. What can a police officer do if the driver refuses to stop? The answer is nothing short of forcible stop technique or continue the pursuit until there is an accident. Does it make sense and pass the reasonable man's test to continue a pursuit that risks death or serious injury, especially when the risks outweigh the benefits. Any police officer who continues a pursuit after the driver demonstrates that they will not stop should be asked: What was your plan?, Why did you keep chasing the suspect?, and What did you expect would happen? The chances are great that they will be asked these questions, if not by a supervisor, then in court.

Chapter 8

THIRD QUESTION–WHEN TO ABANDON THE PURSUIT–TERMINATION EQUATION

An officer should not be reprimanded for terminating a pursuit; however, disciplinary action is justifiable for officers exercising poor judgement in continuing a pursuit. (Sergeant Les Abbott, "Pursuit Driving," FBI Bulletin, November, 1988.)

Sergeant Abbott's statement is applicable today, maybe even more so. Once the pursuit has started, the officer must at all times use his/her best judgement, buttressed by training and policy, in evaluating and reevaluating the pursuit and make a continuous appraisal in deciding to continue. As I have repeatedly said, the element of personal challenge should never enter into this decision. More often than not, the decision to abandon the pursuit is, under most circumstances, the proper course of action. As I said earlier, if neither driver (officer or violator) voluntarily or involuntarily (run out of gas, mechanical failure) chooses to terminate the pursuit, there are only two possible outcomes–the violator escapes or there is an accident. Pursuits are to terminated when:

1. **The *known* risks involved outweigh the benefits to be gained.**
2. **Conditions clearly indicate the futility of further pursuit.**
3. **The offense is a misdemeanor and the identity of the violator is known.**
4. **The pursuing officer knows, or has reason to believe, that (1), the fleeing vehicle is operated by a juvenile who has committed a misdemeanor or a non-violent felony, and (2), safety factors involved are obviously greater than a juvenile can cope with.**
5. **Directed to by any shift supervisor or others in authority.**

Known Risks Outwiegh Benefits

The most frequently cited reason (in policies I have reviewed and research studies I have examined) to abandon a pursuit is when the known risks outweigh the benefits to be gained by continuing the pursuit. This led me to develop what I call the **Termination Equation** (Barker, 1996).

At this point I should mention, that I and numerous others who write research and testify on pursuit have been criticized for leisurely Monday Morning Quarterbacking the split-second decisions of officers in the field. My response has been, and still is, that there are few split-second decisions in police work [reflex action shootings may be an exception].

We know to a "moral certainty" (to borrow a term from the U.S. Supreme Court) that law enforcement officers will engage in certain activities during their routine duties: stop suspects; arrest suspects; search suspects; search houses and vehicles; interrogate suspects; handle domestic violence calls; deal with special populations–drunk, sick, mentally ill; use deadly and nondeadly force; use firearms; stop vehicles and engage in pursuits.

The constitutions and laws at the federal and state level control the behavior of police officers as they go about these duties. Written policies, procedures and rules should be promulgated by individual police agencies to define and, even, restrict the activities of police officers as they perform these "moral certainty" duties. Furthermore, officers must be trained and retrained in these "moral certainty" duties. In my opinion, the "split-second" argument applied to these duties is an excuse for inaction. Those that evoke the "split-second" myth do so to excuse their own inaction or to confuse those unfamiliar with police work.

The Termination Equation

The **Termination Equation** should be understood as the justification for pursuit balanced against the initiating offense, the need for immediate apprehension, and the risks involved.

Justification for Pursuit = Initiating Offense
+ Need for Immediate Apprehension
+ Risks Involved

Law enforcement officers must understand that any pursuit can be terminated, many should be terminated and all should be terminated when the risks involved outweighs the need for immediate apprehension.

Initiating Offense

As we have seen, the initiating offense for the majority of all police pursuits is the commission of a traffic violation. Therefore, the **known** initiating offense in most pursuits is a traffic violation and they are of a hazardous or nonhazardous nature. The agency's policy, and attendant procedures, rules and regulations, should clearly indicate that the justification for pursuit is based on known events and not speculation. Auten (1994) calls into question the need for pursuit of a common nonhazardous violation.

Officer Observes a Driver Run Stop Sign– Completed Violation

1. Many officers routinely ignore such violations unless they are extremely flagrant;
2. Such violations occur undetected on a frequent basis with no adverse consequences;
3. The traffic collision probability because of the violation (actual number of total violations: traffic collisions) is very low;
4. And, one in three pursuits results in a traffic collision.

Alpert and Madden (1994) question the need for unsafe (risks outweigh benefits) pursuits for hazardous violators, viz., DUI. They state that a drunk driver poses a serious risk to all motorists and must be stopped. However, if he/she will not stop, a chase often poses a greater risk than the drunk driver. They point out that there is nothing short of deadly force that the police can do to stop a driver who will not pull over. Therefore, "Perhaps, the only thing more dangerous than a drunk driver on the road is a drunk driver being chased by the police." (Alpert & Madden, 1994:43). Driving abilities and reasoning functions dulled by alcohol or drugs create a huge potential for disaster during a high-speed pursuit.

Even if the known initiating offense is misdemeanor or felony, the officer must balance the offense against the need for immediate apprehension and risks involved. Is it worth the possibility of death or serious injury to violators, officers or the public to pursue a shoplifter, a minor property offender, someone who has driven off without paying for gas, a forger, a stolen car driver, a robber, a murderer? This question must be asked no matter what the violation. And, it will be asked if there is an accident with deaths or injuries.

Need for Immediate Apprehension

Closely related to the known initiating offense is the need for immediate apprehension. The known initiating offense along with the information about the driver, the vehicle and the occupants are factored into the Termination Equation to determine the need for immediate apprehension. The more that is known, the less is the need for immediate apprehension.

If the identity of the violator is known or strongly suspected and the known initiating offense is a traffic violation, a misdemeanor or a nonlife-threatening felony; then pursuits (especially prolonged high speed pursuits) under unsafe conditions are not justified. Remember the reasonable and prudent man standard.

Questions to be considered are: Is there an overriding need to take immediate action or is there a reasonable expectation that safer alternatives are available? Can a warrant be secured? Can a B.O.L.O. be dispatched? Will the violator resume safe driving habits if the pursuit is terminated by the officer. Will the violator stop and abandon the vehicle. Obviously, the officer can not answer these questions. However, should he or she be given the opportunity? Does the possibility exist that the violator can be arrested or stopped under safer conditions later?

On occasion, officers have stopped vehicles, secured tag number, made eyeball observations of driver and occupants, obtained driver's licenses or other forms of identification prior to initiating a pursuit.

I am aware of a traffic pursuit that led to an accident and the deaths of two teenage girls and their two babies under two years-old where the officer positively knew the driver and was aware of the occupants. He had stopped the vehicle on a traffic violation, secured driver's identification, and decided to make a possible DUI arrest. When the officer attempted to make an arrest, the driver jumped back into the vehicle and drove off. Assisting officers from another jurisdiction set up what was, in effect, a "deadman's roadblock." The violator didn't stop and hit a tree. Unfortunately, it is not uncommon for violators to attempt to flee, even after being identified, when they are told they are under arrest. Officers who chase under these circumstances do so because of personal challenge or getting even.

It is common knowledge among police officers that more people go to jail for "Contempt of Cop" (COP) or POP–"Pissing off the Police," than for any other reason. Police officers exercise a great deal of discretion in deciding whether or not to make an arrest or issue a citation. Those who disrespect the officer or challenge his/her authority are more likely to be arrested or get a citation. A pursuit should never be undertaken and continued because the officer is "ticked off" or trying to teach someone a lesson.

Through the years, I have been told numerous "war stories" of pursuits where the identity of the violator was known to a certainty or highly suspected. Nevertheless, the officers initiated a pursuit or continued an unsafe pursuit, some of which ended in deaths or injuries. When asked why they pursued, the answer was usually an incredulous "We couldn't let the dirt bag get away with running from us."

Closely related to this are the high numbers of drivers injured after the pursuit has ended. Many law enforcement officers and executives feigned surprise at the beating of Rodney King at the end of his pursuit. I was not surprised and I would suspect that the majority of police officers or ex-police officers who saw the videotape were not surprised. One-third of the injuries in the 323 pursuits studied by Alpert and Dunham (1988) occurred after the pursuit was terminated. Most of the injuries (87%) were only minor scratches, cuts and bruises. However, 1.4 percent were lifethreatening and 3 percent were deaths.

Instructors from the Federal Law Enforcement Training Center (1984) stated:

> There have been instances where the adrenalin has not shut off once the fleeing suspect has been stopped and law enforcement officers have been known to overreact while still fueled by the excitement of the chase. Complaints of undue force are not unknown at the end of such chases. While such overreaction can be understood, it cannot be condoned. The purpose of the supervisor on the scene will prevent adverse actions arising out of the pursuit situation. (Epstein et al., 1984)

Some departments have even gone so far as to recommend that the driver of the primary chase vehicle not arrest the driver:

Apprehension of Suspect(s):

1. After a vehicular pursuit has ended and the suspects are being apprehended it is preferable that the driver of the primary vehicle **NOT** arrest or take into custody the driver of the vehicle.
2. If possible, an officer from a back-up unit or the nondriving officer in the primary vehicle shall physically take the suspect(s) into custody. (Bessemer, Alabama PD Policy)

Having a supervisor present at the termination point is certainly a good procedure for policy agencies to adopt. Although the presence of a supervisor at the Rodney King incident made a bad situation worse, the control exercised by a supervisor can ensure that policies, procedures and rules are followed.

Known Risks

The known risks include all the limiting factors discussed under the decision of when to pursue: known initiating offense; the roadway and traffic conditions; police vehicle type and condition; the time of day and geographic conditions; availability or lack of assistance; and possibility of alternative actions. The officer makes his/her decision on an analysis of whether the speed is dangerous and exceeds the flow of traffic, the likelihood of pedestrian and vehicular traffic, the erratic behavior of the violator after the pursuit began: driving the wrong way on one-way streets, driving without lights, driving over curbs or through private property, the driver is a juvenile, and whether or not there exists a clear and unreasonable hazard to others if the pursuit continues. Ultimately, the decision rests on the question–Is an accident foreseeable if the pursuit continues. If the answer is yes, terminate the pursuit. Remember, if neither party (officer or violator) terminates the pursuit, there are only two possibilities–the violator escapes or there is an accident.

The known risks present risks of injury and death to: (1) the driver of the pursued vehicle; (2) the occupants of the pursued vehicle; (3)others using the highways as drivers, occupants, or pedestrians; (4)officers actively engaged in the pursuit or those coming to assist.

Although the pursuing officer/s may dismiss the risk to the driver as one he/she willingly chooses when attempting to elude, law enforcement officers have an obligation to the driver if it is in their power, or at least not increase the risk of death or injury to that person. For example, the driver may be a juvenile who committed a traffic offense, a misdemeanor, or nonthreatening felony. That young driver may be fleeing because he/she fears the worst possible punishment that may happen–Mamma or Daddy is going to ground him or her if they are caught. Is it worth the risk of death or injury to the violator or his passengers to write a traffic citation, make a misdemeanor arrest, or even a felony arrest under these circumstances?

As previously stated, the risk of death or injury to a pursued vehicle's occupants deserves special attention. The pursuing officer has an obligation, maybe even a duty, to lessen or negate their risks of harm. Often, the occupants are innocent parties who have had the misfortune of being in a car whose driver decides to elude the police. This is particularly true for children below the age of consent.

The officer must also consider that those of the age of consent may be unwilling occupants, especially after a pursuit begins. They may be telling the driver to stop or let them out and he/she will not comply.

In evaluating the known risk, the officer should understand that conditions during a pursuit must be constantly evaluated and terminated whenever the risks become greater than the benefits to be gained by continuing the chase. There is nothing wrong with terminating a dangerous pursuit even when later apprehension may be remote. And, I should stress that termination means termination.

I have often heard on TV, in court and also read in newspapers and depositions, "I "backed off" just before the accident," or "our officer backed off the chase just before... However, I have never seen a definition of "backing-off" in any policy I have read. I have not seen it defined in any research study or the professional literature. My experience with this term leads me to conclude that it is an overused CYA technique to justify a pursuit that should have been terminated prior to an accident, but wasn't. If the pursued vehicle can see the emergency lights and hear the siren he/she is being actively pursued no matter how close the police vehicle is.

Termination of a pursuit means that the pursuing vehicle(s) has turned off all emergency equipment and resumed safe, legal speed. This sends the message to the violator that he/she is no longer being actively pursued. Two good examples of termination appear in the policies of two Alabama police agencies.

> Pursuits shall be terminated by stopping the police vehicle at an intersection, turning off the roadway and then deactivating the emergency lights and siren, and then radio your location; the last known location of the vehicle and then return to your patrol area. Jacksonville Police Department, Jacksonville, Alabama.

> Termination of Pursuit-A pursuit shall terminate when the primary officer turns off the emergency equipment, resumes routine vehicle operation and informs dispatch. Bessemer Police Department, Bessemer, Alabama.

Alpert has also stated:

> Once a decision has been made that the risks of the pursuit outweigh the benefits, all emergency warning equipment must be deactivated to give the pursued the message that he is no longer being actively pursued (Alpert, Sept/Oct 1988).

At this point, the questions arises–If I terminate the pursuit and the violator continues to drive in an unsafe manner and has an accident with injuries and/or deaths will I get sued. My answer is–probably. Will the suit be successful–No. Remember, I said that the officer makes his or her decision based on known events, not speculation. If the officer, based on known risks, decides that the pursuit is too dangerous to continue, he or she is following agency policy, accepted police standards and practices, and legal precedent contained in court decisions. He/she has made a correct and wise decision. As Urbonya (1991) points out:

> A decision not to pursue [or terminate a pursuit], however, does not subject police officers to liability because, as the DeShaney Court determined, there is no general duty to protect the public from harm caused by third parties (DeShaney, 489 U.S. at 200-01). A duty arises only if the harmed

person was in the custody of the officers. When police officers decide not to pursue, they are not liable for the harm caused by the unapprehended driver to other motorists and pedestrians because the injured individuals were not in the custody of officers.

The **Termination Equation** must be applied to all pursuits. The agency's written directive system–policies, procedures and rules–must clearly indicate that the *justification for any pursuit* must be based on the *known initiating offense*, the *need* for *immediate apprehension*, balanced against the *known risks*. Training must emphasize that the decision to pursue or continue a pursuit is based on known events and not speculation. Balancing the benefits against the risks is the only way to ensure that whatever pursuits are conducted are as safe as possible. Now, let's apply the questions–when to pursue; what to do, or not do, during a pursuit; and when to abandon the pursuit–Termination Equation–to the chase in Chapter 1.

Chapter 9

RODNEY ROOKIE'S FIRST CHASE REVISITED

Before we revisit Rodney Rookie's first chase, I should tell you that the events described are true, only the names have been changed to protect the guilty. The initiating offense was a traffic violation. Rodney and his partner, Ted Brown, saw the blue T-Bird run a red light at Avenue I. According to the hazardous, nonhazardous violation distinction we drew in Chapter 6, how would you classify the initiating offense? What Rodney and Ted saw was a vehicle running the red light, a nonhazardous completed violation. They did not see the T-Bird before it ran the red light. They did not *know* how the driver was going to drive after running the light. What is the benefit to be gained by stopping the violator? Should they have attempted a traffic stop? Should they have engaged in a pursuit if the traffic stop was not successful? We must examine the other limiting factors before answering these questions.

When the violation occurred, it was six o'clock in the evening at a traffic light controlling access from one strip shopping mall to another. Time of day, geographic location, and the amount of vehicular and pedestrian traffic combined to create an extremely dangerous situation. Consider the emotional state of the driver, Ted Brown. He was ticked off. Brown turns on his emergency equipment and the T-Bird accelerates and increases the distance between him and the police vehicle. Some may say that we now have a hazardous violation. One representing a continuing danger to the public, running a red light and speeding. This is true. However, when a new, not the initiating violation, is committed by a fleeing suspect, as they always are, the officer must examine the extent to which the new violation was caused by the pursuit itself.

The officer must also evaluate the increased *known* risk associated with the new violation causes and the likelihood of additional violations. In this case, the violator was not speeding until the emergency equipment was turned on. Ted Brown attempted a traffic stop and it was not successful. Ted Brown decided to pursue? Now we have two speeding vehicles in a congested mall area at six PM.

Ted Brown had to accelerate to 70 mph in a 25 mile zone to attempt to catch-up to the T-Bird. Ted also wove in and out of the traffic to catchup. At times, Ted driving with his emergency equipment engaged, passed slower moving vehicles on the right, and sometimes he was in the oncoming lanes of traffic. The two speeding vehicles are passing fast food restaurants, service stations, frightened pedestrians holding packages and small children, cars stopped in the middle of the road, and some pulled over. Do the benefits to be gained by continuing the pursuit outweigh the risks? What are the benefits of continuing the pursuit? If the violator stops, Ted will cite him for speeding and running a red light. Or maybe, Ted will arrest him for eluding a police officer and reckless driving. What are the risks involved? Under these circumstances any reasonable person, let alone a trained police officer, knows that if the pursuit continues there is going to be an accident. Any reasonable person also know that at these speeds; seventy-miles per hour, the resulting accident is going to cause serious injury and/or death.

The T-Bird turns into a residential neighborhood and the driver continues to attempt to elude Brown who follows and duplicates the erratic driving of the T-Bird. At Avenue and 16th street, the police vehicle is only one-half car length behind the T-Bird. What would happen if the T-Bird's driver decided to stop? Is Ted Brown pushing or pursuing the driver. Do you think that, maybe, Ted Brown has fallen victim to pursuit fixation?

Even when the pursuit is over Ted Brown is unable to control his emotions. The teenager pulls over and becomes a police brutality victim. He also enlists Rodney Rookie into the cover-up of his misconduct.

If we apply the **Termination Equation** to this particular chase, what can we learn. First, I would argue that there should never have been a pursuit. The *known* initiating offense balanced against the *known* risks weighed heavily against pursuit. A reasonable person, especially a trained law enforcement officer, would know that. However, a pursuit did take place. When should it have been terminated by the police driver. The pursuit should have been terminated at Avenue I and 13th street. The T-Bird ran another light and turned into a residential neighborhood. Brown knows, or should have known, that the violator is not going to stop and he is heading into a residential neighborhood. The risks of an accident with serious injury and death are overwhelming.

The fact that there was no accident and that the driver did eventually pull over should not be seen as justifications for this pursuit. As sometimes happens, good luck rides the pursuit route. On the other hand, when bad luck combines with a lack of guidance, policies, procedures, and rules; a lack of training; uncontrolled emotions; bad judgment; and faulty decisionmaking; unsafe pursuits occur and someone is seriously injured or killed. Then, someone is sued.

Well-regulated safe pursuits may be necessary. However, every law enforcement agency at all levels of government, federal, state and local, should develop restrictive policies governing emergency vehicle operations (emergency calls and pursuit) along with sanctions for those not adhering to the written directive system. These same agencies should ensure that all personnel understand the pursuit written directives and are trained and retrained in emergency vehicle operations. The policies and training should address the three questions; when to pursue, what to do, or not do during pursuit, and when to abandon the pursuit. Law enforcement officers should understand the **Termination Equation**. They should be trained in its use. Supervisors should apply the **Termination Equation** to all pursuits that occur in their agency. This will lead to restrictive policies and increased training and eventually safer and less pursuits. As I said at the end of Chapter 2, *the days of unrestricted high-speed pursuit, especially for traffic violations, are over.* Some law enforcement officers and their agencies do not know it yet, but they are quickly finding it out.

REFERENCES

Abbott, Les (1988), Pursuit Driving. *FBI Law Enforcement Bulletin,* (November, 1988).

Alpert, Geoffrey P. (1988). Police Pursuits-Linking Data to Decisions. *Criminal Law Bulletin,* (Vol 24, No. 5, Sept/Oct, 1988).

Alpert, Geoffrey P. & Lorie Fridell (1992). *Police Vehicles and Deadly Force: Instruments of Deadly Force.* Prospect Heights, IL: Waveland Press.

_______& Thomas Madden(1994). Police Pursuit Driving: An Empirical Analysis of Critical Decisions. *American Journal of Police,* (Vol. XIII, No.4, 1994).

Auten, James (1985). Law Enforcement Driving-Part II: Emergency Driving. *Law and Order,* (June, 1985).

_______(1985). Law Enforcement Driving-Part III: Pursuit Driving. *Law and Order,* (July, 1985).

_______(1988). Law Enforcement Driving: Forcible Stop Techniques. *Law and Order* (October, 1988)

Auten, James H. (1989). *Law Enforcement Driving.* Springfield, IL.: Charles C Thomas.

_______(1994). Initiating Events in Pursuit. *Law and Order,* (October, 1994).

Barker, Tom (1984), Police Pursuit Driving: The Need for Policy. *Police Chief.* (July, 1984).

_______(1996). Making Pursuits Safer: The Termination Equation helps officers end dangerous pursuits. *Law and Order.* (March, 1996).

Bayley, David H. (1994). *Police for the Future.* New York:Oxford University Press.

Brower v. *County of Inyo,* 489 U.S. (1989)-Slip Opinion.

City of Canton v. *Harris,* No. 86-1088, U.S. (1989)-Slip Opinion.

California Highway Patrol (1983). *Pursuit Study.* State of California.

delCarmen, Rolando (1991). *Civil Liabilities in Law Enforcement. A Text For Law Enforcement.* Englewood Cliffs NJ: Brady.

Epstein, David G. et. al. (1984). Pursuit Driving: A Matter of Selection, Training and Supervision. *The National Sheriff,* (January, 1984).

Hannigan, Maurice J. (1992). The Visibility of Police Pursuit. *Police Chief,* (February 1992).

Hoy, V.L. (1982). Research and Planning, in B. Garmire ed. *Local Government Public Management,* 2nd ed. Washington, D.C.: International City Management Association.

International Association of Chiefs of Police (nd). Emergency Calls. Training Key 113. Gaithersburg, Md.:IACP

_______(nd). Emergency Vehicle Operations–Policy and Procedures. Training Key 271. Gaithersburg, Md.:IACP.

_______(1989). Vehicular Pursuit-Model Policy. *A Compilation of Model Policies,* Gaithersburg, Md.: IACP.

International Association of Directors of Law Enforcement Standards and Training, (1989) *Guidelines for the Evaluation and Structuring of a Driver Training Process for Law Enforcement Personnel.* U.S. Department of Transportation: National Highway Traffic Safety Administration.

Law Enforcement Officer's Manual (nd). Office of the Attorney General: State of Maine

Mayo, Louis. *Law Enforcement News,* May 31, 1989:13.

McGue, Keller M. & Tom Barker (1996). Emergency Response and Pursuit Issues in Alabama. *American Journal of Police,* (Vol. XV, No. 4, 1996).

Minnesota Board of Peace Officers Standards and Training (1988). In Alpert, Geoffrey P. & Lori Fridell (1992).

Mobile, Alabama Police Department (May 1988). Police Academy Handout #PGO 34A:3.

National Committee on Uniform Traffic Laws and Ordinances (1987). *Uniform Vehicle Code and Model Traffic Ordinances.* Evanston, IL.

National Highway Traffic Safety Administration (1994). *Fatal Accident Reporting System Reports.*

Schofield, Daniel L. (1988). Legal Issues of Pursuit Driving. *FBI Law Enforcement Bulletin,* (May, 1988).

Schultz, Donald O. (1979). *Police Pursuit Driving Handbook.* Houston, TX: Gulf Publishing Co.

Tennessee v. *Garner,* 471 U.S. 1 (1985).

Urbonya, Kathryn R. (1991). The Constitutionality of High-Speed Pursuits Under the Fourth and Fourteenth Amendments. *Saint Louis University Law Journal,* (Vol. 35-205).

U.S. Department of Justice (1987). *Deadly Force Policy Development and Implementation Workshop for Police Executives.* Bureau of Justice Assistance.

Whetsel, John & J.W. Bennett (1992). Pursuits: a deadly Force Issue. *Police Chief,* (February, 1992).

Appendix A

NOTICE: This Opinion is subject to formal revision before publication in the preliminary print of the United States Reports. Readers are requested to notify the Reporter of decisions, Supreme Court of the United States, Washington, D.C. 20543, of any typographical or other formal errors, in order that corrections may be made before the preliminary print goes to press.

SUPREME COURT OF THE UNITED STATES

No. 87–248

GEORGIA BROWER, INDIVIDUALLY AND AS ADMINISTRATOR OF THE ESTATE OF WILLIAM JAMES CALDWELL (BROWER), DECEASED, ET AL., PETITIONERS *V.* COUNTY OF INYO ET AL.

ON WRIT OF CERTIORARI TO THE UNITED STATES COURT OF APPEALS FOR THE NINTH CIRCUIT

[March 21, 1989]

JUSTICE SCALIA delivered the opinion of the Court.

On the Night of October 23, 1984, William James Caldwell (Brower) was killed when the stolen car that he had been driving at high speeds for approximately 20 miles in an effort to elude pursuing police crashed into a police roadblock. His heirs, the petitioners here, brought this action in Federal District Court under 42 U.S.C.§ 1983, claiming *inter alia* that respondents used "brutal, excessive, unreasonable and unnecessary physical force" in establishing the roadblock, and thus effected an unreasonable seizure of Brower, in violation of the Fourth Amendment. Petitioners alleged that "under color of statutes, regulations, customs and usages," respondents (1) caused an 18 wheel tractor-trailer to be placed across both lanes of a two-lane highway in the path of Brower's flight, (2) "effectively concealed" this roadblock by placing it behind a curve and leaving it unilluminated, and (3) positioned a police car, with its headlight on, between Brower's oncoming vehicle and the truck, so that Brower would be "blinded" on his approach. App. 8–9. Petitioners further alleged that Brower's fatal collision with the truck was "a proximate result" of this official conduct. *Id.*, at 9. The District Court granted respondents' motion to dismiss the complaint for failure to state a claim on the ground (insofar as the Fourth Amendment claim was concerned) that "establishing a roadblock [was] not unreasonable under the circumstances." App. to Pet. for Cert. A–21. A divided panel of the Court of Appeals for the Ninth Circuit affirmed the dismissal of the Fourth Amendment claim on the basis that no "seizure" had occurred. 817 F. 2d 540, 545–546 (1987). We granted certiorari, 487 U.S.–(1988), to resolve a conflict between that decision and the contrary holding of the Court of Appeals for the Fifth Circuit in *Jamieson* v. *Shaw*, 772 F. 1205 (1985).

The Fourth Amendment to the Constitution provides:

> "The right of the people to be secure in their persons, houses, papers, and effects, against unreasonable searches and seizures, shall not be violated, and no Warrants shall issue, but upon probable cause, supported by Oath or affirmation, and particularly describing the place to be searched, and the person or things to be seized."

In *Tennessee* v. *Garner*, 471 U.S. 1 (1985), we concluded unanimously that a police officer's fatal shooting of a fleeing suspect constituted Fourth Amendment "seizure." See *id.*, at 7; *id.*, at 25 (O'CONNER, J., dissenting.) We reasoned that "[w]henever an officer restrains the freedom of a person to walk away, he has seized that person." *Id.*, at 7. While acknowledging *Garner*, the Court of Appeals here concluded here that no "seizure" occurred when Brower collided with the police roadblock because "[p]rior to his failure to stop voluntarily, his freedom of movement was never arrested or restrained" and because "[h]e had a number of opportunities to stop his automobile prior to the impact." 817 F. 2d, at 546. Essentially the same thing, however, could have been said in *Garner*. Brower's independent decision to continue the chase can no more eliminate respondents' responsibility for the termination of his movement effected by the roadblock than Garner's independent decision to flee eliminated the Memphis police officer's responsibility for the termination of his movement effected by the bullet.

The Court of Appeals was impelled to its result by consideration of what it described as the "analogous situation" of a police chase in which the suspect unexpectedly loses control of his car and crashes. See *Galas* v. *McKee,* 801 F. 2d 200, 202–203 (CA6 1986) (no seizure in such circumstances). We agree that no unconstitutional seizure occurred there, but not for a reason that has any application to the present case. Violation of the Fourth Amendment requires intentional acquisition of physical control. A seizure occurs even when an unintended person or thing is the object of the detention or taking, see *Hill* v. *California*, 401 U.S. 797, 802–805 (1971); cf. *Maryland* v. *Garrison*, 480 U.S. 79, 85–89 (1987), but the detention or taking itself must be willful. This is implicit to the word "seizure," which can hardly be applied to an unknowing act. The writs of assistance that were the principal grievance against which the Fourth Amendment was directed, see *Boyd* v. *United States,* 116 U.S. 616 , 624–625 (1886); T. Cooley, Constitutional Limitations *301–*302, did not involve unintended consequences of government action. Nor did the general warrants issued by Lord Halifax in the 1760's, which produced "the first and only litigation in the English courts in the field of search and seizure," T. Taylor, Two Studies in Constitutional Interpretation 26 (1969), including the case we have described as a "monument of English freedom" "undoubtedly familiar" to "every American statesman" at the time the constitution was adopted, and considered to be "the true and ultimate expression of constitutional law," 116 U.S., at 626 (discussing *Entick* v. *Carrington,* 19 How. St. Tr. 1029, 95 Eng. Rep. 807 (K. B. 1765)). In sum, the Fourth Amendment addresses "misuse of power," *Byars* v. *United States,* 273 U.S. 28, 33 (1927), not the accidental effects of otherwise lawful government conduct.

Thus, if a parked and unoccupied police car slips its brake and pins a passerby against wall, it is likely that a tort has occurred, but not a violation of the Fourth Amendment. And the situation would not change if the passerby happened, by lucky chance, to be a serial murderer for whom there was an outstanding warrant–even if, at the time he was thus pinned, he was in the process of running away from two pursuing constables. It is clear , in other words, that a Fourth Amendment seizure does not occur whenever there is a governmentally caused termination of an individual's freedom of movement (the innocent passerby), nor even when there is a governmentally caused and governmentally *desired* termination of an individual's freedom of movement (the fleeing felon), but only when there is a governmental termination of freedom of movement *through means intentionally applied.* That is the reason there was no seizure in the hypothetical situation that concerned the Court of Appeals. The pursuing police car sought to stop the suspect by the show of authority represented by flashing lights and continued pursuit; and though he was in fact stopped by a different means–his loss of control of his vehicle and the subsequent crash. If, instead of that, the police cruiser had pulled alongside the fleeing car and sideswiped it, then the termination of the suspects movement would have been a seizure.

This analysis is reflected by our decision in *Hester* v. *United States,* 265 U.S. 57(1924), where an armed revenue agent had pursued the defendant and his accomplice after seeing them obtain containers thought to be filled with "moonshine whiskey." During their flight they dropped the containers which the agent recovered. The defendant sought to suppress testimony concerning the containers' contents as the product of an unlawful seizure. Justice Holmes, speaking for unanimous Court, concluded: "The defendants own acts, and those of his associates, disclosed the jug, the jar and the bottle–and there was no seizure in the sense of the law when the officers examined the contents of each after they had been abandoned." *Id.,* at 58. Thus even though the incriminating containers were unquestionably taken into possession as a result (in the broad sense) of action by the police, the Court held that no seizure had taken place. It would have been quite different, of course, if the revenue agent had shouted "Stop and give us those bottles, in the name of the law!" and the defendant and his accomplice had complied. Then the taking of possession would have been not merely the result of government action but the very means(the show of authority) that the government selected,and a Fourth Amendment seizure would have occurred.

In applying these principles to the dismissal of petitioners' Fourth Amendment complaint for failure to state a claim, we can sustain the District Court's action only if, taking the allegations of the complaint in the light most favorable to the petitioners, see *Scheuer* v. *Rhodes,* 416 U. S. 232, 236 (1974), we could nonetheless conclude that they could prove no set of facts entitling them to relief for a "seizure." See *Conley* v. *Gibson,* 355 U. S. 41, 45–46 (1957). Petitioners have alleged the establishment of a roadblock crossing both lanes of the highway. In marked contrast to a police car pursuing with flashing lights, or to a policeman in the road signaling an oncoming car to halt, see *Kibbe* v. *Springfield,* 777 F. 2d 801, 802–803 (CA1 1985), cert. dism'd, 480 U. S. 257 (1987), a roadblock is not just a significant show of authority to induce a voluntary stop, but is designed to produce a stop by physical impact if voluntary compliance does not occur. It may well be that respondents here preferred, and indeed earnestly hoped, that

Brower would stop on his own, without striking the barrier, but we do not think it practicable to conduct such an inquiry into subjective intent. See *United States* v. *Leon*, 468 U. S. 897, 922, n. 23 (1984); see also *Anderson* v. *Creighton*, 483 U. S. 635, 641 (1987); *Harlow* v. *Fitzgerald*, 457 U. S. 800, 815–819 (1982). Nor do we think it possible, in determining whether there has been a seizure in a case such as this, to distinguish between a roadblock that is designed to give the oncoming driver the option of a voluntary stop (*e.g.*, one at the end of a long straightaway), and a roadblock that is designed precisely to produce a collision (*e.g.*, one located just around a bend). In determining whether the means that terminates the freedom of movement is the very means that the government intended we cannot draw too fine a line, or we will be driven to saying that one is not seized who has been stopped by the accidental discharge of a gun with which he was meant only to be bludgeoned, or by a bullet in the heart which was meant only for the leg. We think it enough for a seizure that a person be stopped. by the very instrumentality set in motion or put in place in order to achieve that result. It was enough here, therefore, that, according to the allegations of the complaint, Brower was meant to be stopped by the physical obstacle of the roadblock–and that he was so stopped.

This is not to say that the precise character of the roadblock is irrelevant to further issues in this case. "Seizure" alone is not enough for § 1983 liability; the seizure must be "unreasonable." Petitioners can claim the right to recover for Brower's death only because the unreasonableness they allege consists precisely of setting up the roadblock in such manner as to be likely to kill him. This should be contrasted with the situation that would obtain if the sole claim of unreasonableness were that there was no probable cause for the stop. In that case, Brower had had the opportunity to stop voluntarily at the roadblock, but had negligently or intentionally driven into it, then, because of lack of proximate causality, respondents, though responsible for depriving him of his freedom of movement, would not be liable for his death. See *Martinez* v. *California*, 444 U. S. 277, 285 (1980); *Cameron* v. *Pontiac*, 813 F. 2d 786 (CA6 1987). Thus, the circumstances of this roadblock, including the allegation that headlights were used to blind the oncoming driver, may yet determine the outcome of this case.

The complaint here sufficiently alleges that respondents, under color of law, sought to stop Brower by means of a roadblock and succeeded in doing so. That is enough to constitute a "seizure" within meaning of the Fourth Amendment. Accordingly, we reverse the judgement of the Court of Appeals, and remand for consideration of whether the District Court properly dismissed the Fourth Amendment claim on the basis that the alleged roadblock did not effect a seizure that was "unreasonable."

It is so ordered.

SUPREME COURT OF THE UNITED STATES

No. 87–248

GEORGIA BROWER, INDIVIDUALLY AND AS ADMINISTRATOR OF THE ESTATE OF WILLIAM JAMES CALDWELL (BROWER), DECEASED, ET AL., PETITIONERS *V.* COUNTY OF INYO ET AL.

ON WRIT OF CERTIORARI TO THE UNITED STATES COURT OF APPEALS FOR THE NINTH CIRCUIT

[March 21, 1989]

JUSTICE STEVENS, with whom JUSTICE BRENNAN, JUSTICE MARSHALL, and JUSTICE BLACKMUN join, concurring in the judgement.

The Court is unquestionably correct in concluding that respondents' use of a roadblock to stop Brower's car constituted a seizure within the meaning of the Fourth Amendment. I therefore concur in its judgement. I do not, however, join in its opinion because its dicta seem designed to decide a number of cases not before the Court and to establish the proposition that "[v]iolation of the Fourth Amendment requires an intentional acquisition of physical control." *Ante*, at 3.

The intentional acquisition of physical control of something is no doubt a characteristic of the typical seizure, but I am not entirely sure that it is an essential element of every seizure or that this formulation is particularly helpful in deciding close cases. The Court suggests that the test it articulates does not turn on the subjective intent of the officer. *Ante*, at 5. This, of course, not only comports with the recent trend in our cases, see, *e.g.*, *Harlow* v. *Fitzgerald*, 457 U. S. 800, 815–819 (1982); *United States* v. *Mendenhall*, 446 U. S. 544, 554, n. 6 (1980) (opinion of Stewart, J.), but also makes perfect sense. No one would suggest that the Fourth Amendment provides no protection against a police officer who is too drunk to act intentionally, yet who appears in uniform brandishing a weapon in a threatening manner. Alternatively, however, the concept of objective intent, at least in the vast majority of cases, adds little to the well-established rule that "a person has been 'seized' within the Fourth Amendment only if, in view of all of the circumstances surrounding the incident, a reasonable person would have believed that he was not free to leave." *Id.*, at 544 (opinion of Stewart, J.); see also *INS* v. *Delgado*, 466 U. S. 210, 215 (1984).

There may be a case that someday comes before this Court in which the concept of the intent is useful in applying the Fourth Amendment. What is extraordinary about the Court's discussion of the intent requirement in this case is that there is no dispute that the roadblock was intended to stop the decedent. Decision in the case before us is thus not advanced by pursuing a hypothetical inquiry concerning whether an unintentional act might also violate the Fourth Amendment. Rather, as explained in Judge Pregerson's dissent in the Court of Appeals, this case is plainly controlled by our decision in *Tennessee* v. *Garner*, 471 U. S. 1 (1985). 817 F. 2d 540, 548 (CA9 1987) (opinion concurring in part and dissenting in part). In that case, we held that "there can be no question that apprehension by the use of deadly force is a seizure subject to the reasonableness requirement of the Fourth Amendment." 471 U. S., at 7. Because it was undisputed that the police officer acted intentionally, we did not discuss the hypothetical case of an unintentional seizure. I would exercise the same restraint here.

I am in full accord with Judge Pregerson's dissenting opinion and, for the reasons stated in his opinion, I join the Court's judgement.

Appendix B

NOTICE: This Opinion is subject to formal revision before publication in the preliminary print of the United States Reports. Readers are requested to notify the Reporter of decisions, Supreme Court of the United States, Washington, D.C. 20543, of any typographical or other formal errors, in order that corrections may be made before the preliminary print goes to press.

SUPREME COURT OF THE UNITED STATES

No. 86–1088

CITY OF CANTON, OHIO, PETITIONER *v.* GERALDINE HARRIS ET AL.

ON WRIT OF CERTIORARI TO THE UNITED STATES COURT OF APPEALS FOR THE SIXTH CIRCUIT

[FEBRUARY 28, 1989]

JUSTICE WHITE delivered the opinion of the Court.

In this case, we are asked to determine if a municipality can ever be liable under 42 U. S. C. § 1983[1] for constitutional violations resulting from its failure to train municipal employees. We hold that, under certain circumstances, such liability is permitted by the statute.

I

In April 1978, respondent Geraldine Harris was arrested by officers of the Canton Police Department. Harris was brought to the police station in a patrol wagon.

When she arrived at the station, Harris was found sitting on the floor of the wagon. She was asked if she needed medical attention,

[1] Title 42 U. S. C. § 1983 provides, in relevant part, that:
"Every person who, under color of any statute, ordinance, regulation, custom, or usage...subjects, or causes to be subjected, any citizen of the United States or other person within the jurisdiction thereof to the deprivation of any rights, privileges, or immunities secured by the Constitution and laws, shall be liable to the party injured in an action at law, suit in equity, or other proper proceeding for redress..."
42 U. S. C. § 1983

responded with an incoherent remark. After she was brought inside the station for processing, Mrs. Harris slumped to the floor on two occasions. Eventually, the police officers left Mrs. Harris lying on the floor to prevent her from falling again. No medical attention was ever summoned for Mrs. Harris. After about an hour, Mrs. Harris was released from custody, and taken by an ambulance (provided by her family) to a nearby hospital. There, Mrs. Harris was diagnosed as suffering from severe emotional ailments; she was hospitalized for one week, and received subsequent outpatient treatment for an additional year.

Some time later, Mrs. Harris commenced this action alleging many state law and constitutional claims against the city of Canton and its officials. Among these claims was one seeking to hold the city liable under 42 U. S. C. § 1983 for its violation of Mrs. Harris' right, under the Due Process Clause of the Fourteenth Amendment, to receive necessary medical attention while in police custody.

A jury trial was held on Mrs. Harris' claims. Evidence was presented that indicated that, pursuant to a municipal regulation,[2] shift commanders were authorized to determine, in their sole discretion, whether a detainee required medical care. Tr. 2–139–2–143. In addition, testimony also suggested that Canton shift commanders were not provided with any special training (beyond first-aid training) to make a determination as to when to summon medical care for an injured detainee. *Ibid.*; App. to Pet. for Cert. 4a.

At the close of the evidence, the District Court submitted the case to the jury, which rejected all of Mrs. Harris' claims except one: Her § 1983 claim against the city resulting from its failure to provide her with medical treatment while in custody. In rejecting the city's subsequent motion for judgement notwithstanding the verdict, the District Court explained the theory of liability as follows:

> "The evidence construed in a manner most favorable to Mrs. Harris could be found by a jury to demonstrate that the City of Canton had a custom or policy of vesting complete authority with the police supervisor of when medical treatment would be administered to prisoners. Further, the jury

[2] The city regulation in question provides that a police officer assigned to act as "jailer" at the City Police Station:

"shall, when a prisoner is found to be unconscious or semi-unconscious, or when he or she is unable to explain his or her condition, or who complains of being ill, have such person taken to hospital for medical treatment, with permission of his supervisor before admitting the person to the City Jail." App. 33.

> could find from the evidence that the vesting of such *carte blanche* authority with the police supervisor without adequate training to recognize when medical treatment is needed was grossly negligent or so reckless that future police misconduct was almost inevitable or substantially certain to result." App. to Pet. for Cert. 16a.

On appeal, the Sixth Circuit affirmed this aspect of the District Court's Analysis, holding that "a municipality is liable for failure to train its police force, [where] the plaintiff...prove[s] that the municipality acted recklessly, intentionally, or with gross negligence." *Id.*, at 5a.[3] The Court of Appeals also stated that an additional prerequisite of this theory of liability was that the plaintiff must prove "that the lack of training was so reckless or grossly negligent that deprivations of persons' constitutional rights were substantially certain to result." *Ibid.* Thus, the Court of Appeals found that there had been no error in submitting Mrs. Harris' "failure to train" claim to the jury. However, the Court of Appeals reversed the judgement for respondent, and remanded this case for a new trial, because it found certain aspects of the District Court's jury instructions might have lead the jury to believe that it could find against the city on a mere *respondeat superior* theory. Because the jury's verdict did not state the basis on which it had ruled for Mrs. Harris on her § 1983 claim, a new trial was ordered.

The city petitioned for certiorari, arguing that the Sixth Circuit's holding represented an impermissible broadening of municipal liability under § 1983. We granted the petition. 485 U. S.–(1988).

II

We first address respondent's contention that the writ of certiorari should be dismissed as improvidently granted, because "petitioner failed to preserve for review the principal issues it now argues in this Court." Brief for Respondent 5.

We think it clear enough that petitioner's three "Questions Presented" in its petition for certiorari encompass the critical question before us in this case: Under what circumstances can inadequate training be found to be "policy" that is actionable under § 1983? See

[3] In upholding Mrs. Harris' "failure to train" claim, the Sixth Circuit relied on two of its previous decisions which had approved such a theory of municipal liability under § 1983. See *Rhymer* v. *Davis*, 754 F. 2d 198 (CA6), vacated and remanded sub nom. *City of Shepherdsville, Ky.* v. *Rhymer*, 473 U. S. 901, reinstated, 775 F. 2d 756, 757 (CA6 1985); *Hayes* v. *Jefferson County, Ky.* 668 F. 2d 869, 874 (CA6 1982).

Pet. for Cert. i. The petition itself addressed this issue directly, attacking the Sixth Circuit's "failure to train" theory as inconsistent with this Court's precedents. See *id.* at 8–12. It is also clear–as respondent conceded at argument, Tr. of Oral Arg. 34, 54–that her Brief in Opposition to our granting of certiorari did not raise the objection that petitioner had failed to press its claims on the courts below.

As to respondent's contention that the claims made by petitioner here were not made in the same fashion below, that failure, if it occurred, does not affect our jurisdiction; and because respondent did not oppose our grant of review at that time based on her contention that these claims were not pressed below, we will not dismiss the writ as improvidently granted. "[T]he 'decision to grant certiorari represents a commitment of scarce judicial resources with a view to deciding the merits...of the questions presented in the petition.'" *St. Louis v. Praprotnik,* 485 U. S.–,–(1988) (quoting *Oklahoma City* v. *Tuttle,* 471 U. S. 808, 816 (1985)). As we have expressly admonished litigants in respondent's position: "No jurisdictional defects of this sort should be brought to our attention *no later* than in respondent's brief in opposition to the petition for certiorari; if not, we considered it within our discretion to deem the defect waived." *Tuttle, supra,* at 816.

It is true that petitioner's litigation posture with respect to the questions presented here has not been consistent; most importantly, petitioner conceded below that "'inadequate training' [is] a means of establishing a municipal liability under Section 1983." Reply Brief for Petitioner 4, n. 3; see also Petition for Rehearing No. 85–3314 (CA6), p. 1. However, at each stage in the proceedings below, petitioner contested any finding of liability on this ground, with objections of varying specificity. It opposed District Court's jury instructions on this issue, Tr. 4–369; claimed in its judgement notwithstanding verdict motion that there was "no evidence of ...policy or practice on the part of the city...[of] den[ying] medical treatment to prisoners," Motion for judgement Notwithstanding Verdict in No. C80–18–A (ND Ohio), p. 1; and argued to the Court of Appeals that there was no basis for finding as policy of denying medical treatment to prisoners in this case. See Brief for Appellant in No. 85–3314 (CA6) pp. 26–29. Indeed, petitioner specifically contended that the Sixth Circuit precedents that permitted inadequate training to be a basis for municipal liability on facts similar to these, see n. 3, *supra,* were in conflict with our decision in *Tuttle*. Brief for Appellant, *supra*, at 29. These various presentations of the issues below might have been so inexact that we would have denied certiorari had this matter been brought our attention at the appropriate stage in the proceedings here. But they were at least adequate to yield a decision by the Sixth Circuit on the questions presented for our review now.

Here the Sixth Circuit held that where a plaintiff proves that a municipality, acting recklessly, intentionally, or with gross negligence, as failed to train its police force–resulting in a deprivation of constitutional rights that was "substantially certain to result"– § 1983 permits that municipality to be held liable for its actions. Petitioners petition for certiorari challenged the soundness of that conclusion, and respondent did not inform us prior to the time that review was granted that petitioner had arguably conceded this point below. Consequently, we will not abstain from addressing the question before us.

III

In *Monell* v. *New York City Dept. of Social Services*, 436 U. S. 658 (1978), we decided that a municipality can be found liable under § 1983 only where the municipality *itself* causes the constitutional violation at issue. *Respondeat superior* or vicarious liability will not attach under § 1983. Id., at 694–695. "It is only when the 'execution of the government's policy or custom...inflicts the injury' that the municipality may be held liable under § 1983. *Springfield, Mass.* v. *Kibbe,* 480 U. S. 257 (1987) (O'CONNOR, J., dissenting) (quoting *Monell*, *supra*, at 694).

Thus, our first inquiry in any case alleging municipal liability under § 1983 is the question of whether there is a direct causal link between a municipal policy or custom, and the alleged constitutional deprivation. The inquiry is a difficult one; one that has left this Court deeply divided in a series of cases that have followed *Monell*;[4] one that is the principal focus of our decision again today.

[4] See, *e. g., St. Louis* v. *Praprotnik*, 485 U. S.––(1988); *Springfield* v. *Kibbe*, 480 U. S. 257 (1987); *Los Angeles* v. *Heller*, 475 U. S. 796 (1986); *Oklahoma City* v. *Tuttle*, 471 U. S. 808 (1985).

A

Based on the difficulty that this case has had defining the contours of municipal liability in these circumstances, petitioner urges us to adopt the rule that a municipality can be found liable under § 1983 only where "the policy in question [is] itself unconstitutional." Brief for Petitioner 15. Whether such a rule is a valid construction of § 1983 is a question the Court has left unresolved. See, *e.g., St. Louis* v. *Praprotnik*, 485 U. S., at –– (BRENNAN, J., concurring in judgement); *Oklahoma City* v. *Tuttle*, 471 U. S., at 824, n. 7. Under such an approach, the outcome here would be rather clear: we would have to reverse and remand the case with instructions that judgement be entered for the petitioner.[5] There can be little doubt that on its face the city's policy regarding medical treatment for detainees is constitutional. The policy states that the City Jailer "shall...have[a person needing medical care] taken to a hospital for medical treatment, with permission from his supervisor..." App. 33. It is difficult to see what constitutional guarantees are violated by such a policy.

Nor, without more, would a city automatically be liable under § 1983 if one of its employees happened to apply the policy in an unconstitutional manner, for liability would then rest on *respondeat superior*. The claim in this case, however, is that if a concededly valid policy is unconstitutionally applied by a municipal employee, the city is liable if the employee has not been adequately trained and the constitutional wrong has been caused by that failure to train. For reasons explained below, we conclude, as have all the Courts of Appeals that

[5] In this Court, in addition to suggesting that the city's failure to train its officers amounted to a "policy" that resulted in the denial of medical care to detainees, respondent also contended the city had a "custom" of denying medical care to those detainees suffering from emotional or mental ailments. See Brief for Respondent 31–32; Tr. of Oral Arg. 38–39. As respondent described in her brief, and at argument, this claim of an unconstitutional "custom" appears to be little more than a restatement of "failure to train as policy" claim. See *Ibid.*

However, to the extant that this claim poses a distinct basis for the city's liability under § 1983, we decline to determine whether respondent's contention that such a "custom" existed is an alternate ground for affirmance. The "custom" claim was not passed on by the Court of Appeals–nor does it appear to have been presented to that court as a distinct ground for its decision. See Brief of Appellee in No. 85–3314 (CA6), pp.4–9, 11. Thus, we will not consider it here.

have addressed this issue,[6] that there are limited circumstances in which an allegation of a "failure to train" can be the basis for liability under § 1983. Thus, we reject petitioner's contention that only unconstitutional policies are actionable under the statute.

B

Though we agree with the court below that a city can be liable under § 1983 for inadequate training of its employees, we cannot agree that the District Court's jury instructions on this issue were proper, for we conclude that the Court of Appeals provided an overly broad rule for when a municipality can be held liable under the "failure to train" theory. Unlike the question of whether a municipality's failure to train employees can ever be a basis for § 1983 liability – on which the Court of Appeals have all agreed, see n. 6, *supra*, – there is substantial division among the lower courts as to what *degree of fault* must be evidenced by the municipality's inaction before liability will be permitted.[7] We hold today that the inadequacy of police training may serve as the basis for § 1983 liability only where the failure to train amounts to deliberate indifference to the rights of persons with

---

[6] In addition to the Sixth Circuit decisions discussed, n. 3, *supra*, most of the other Courts of Appeals have held that a failure to train can create liability under § 1983. See, e. g., *Spell* v. *McDaniel*, 824 F. 2d 1380, 1389–1391 (CA4 1987); *Haynesworth* v. *Miller*, 261 U. S. App. D. C. 66, 80–83, 820 F. 2d 1245, 1259–1262 (1987); *Warren* v. *City of Lincoln, Neb.*, 816 F. 2d 1254, 1262 1263 (CA8 1987); *Bergquist* v. *County of Cochise*, 806 F. 2d 1364, 1369–1370 (CA9 1986); *Wierstak* v. *Heffernan*, 789 F. 2d 968, 974 (CA1 1986); *Fiacco* v. *City of Rensselaer, N. Y.*, 783 F. 2d 319, 326–327 (CA2 1986); *Gilmere* v. *City of Atlanta, Ga.*, 774 F. 2d 1495, 1503–1504 (CA11 1985) (en banc); *Rock* v. *McCoy*, 763 F. 2d 394, 397–398 (CA10 1985); *Languirand* v. *Hayden*, 717 F. 2d 220, 227–228 (CA5 1983). Two other Courts of Appeals have stopped short of expressly embracing this rule, and have instead only implicitly endorsed it. See, *e. g., Colburn* v. *Upper Darby Township*, 838 F. 2d 663, 672–673 (CA3 1988); *Lenard* v. *Argento*, 699 F. 2d 874, 885–887 (CA7 1983).

In addition, six current Members of this Court have joined opinions in the past that have (at least implicitly) endorsed this theory of liability under § 1983. See *Oklahoma* v. *Tuttle, supra*, at 829–831 (Brennan, J., joined by MARSHALL and BLACKMUN, JJ., concurring in part and concurring in judgment); *Springfield* v. *Kibbe*, *supra*, at 268–270. (O'CONNER, J., joined by REHNQUIST, C. J., POWELL and WHITE, JJ., dissenting).

[7] Some courts have held that a showing of "gross negligence" in a city's failure to train its employees is adequate to make out a claim under § 1983. See, *e. g., Bergquist* v. *County of Cochise*, *supra*, at 1370; *Herrera* v. *Valentine*, 653 F. 2d 1220, 1224 (CA8 1981). But the more common rule is that a city must exhibit "deliberate indifference" toward the constitutional rights of persons in its domain before a § 1983 action for "failure to train" is permissible. See, *e. g., Fiacco* v. *City of Rensselaer, supra*, at 326; *Patzner* v. *Burkett*, 779 F. 2d 1363, 1367 (CA8 1985); *Wellington* v. *Daniels*, 717 F. 2d 932, 936 (CA4 1983); *Languirand* v. *Hayden, supra*, at 227.

whom the police come in contact.[8] This rule is most consistent with our admonition in *Monell*, 436 U. S., at 694, and *Polk County* v. *Dodson*, 454 U. S. 312, 326 (1981), that a municipality can be liable under § 1983 only where its policies are the "moving force [behind] the constitutional violation." Only where a municipality's failure to train its employees in a relevant respect evidences a "deliberate indifference" to the rights of its inhabitants can such a shortcoming be properly thought of as a city "policy or custom" that is actionable under § 1983. As in JUSTICE BRENNAN'S opinion in *Pembaur* v. *Cincinnati*, 475 U. S. 469, 483–484 (1986) (plurality) put it: "[M]unicipal liability under § 1983 attaches where–and only where–a deliberate choice to follow a course of action is made from among various alternatives" by city policy makers. See also *Oklahoma City* v. *Tuttle*, 471 U. S. at 823. (opinion of REHNQUIST, J.) Only where a failure to train reflects a "deliberate" or "conscious" choice by a municipality–a "policy" as defined by our prior cases–can a city be liable for such a failure under § 1983.

Monell's rule that a city is not liable under § 1983 unless a municipality cause a constitutional deprivation will not be satisfied by merely alleging that the existing training program for a class of employees, such as police officers, represents a policy for which the city is responsible.[9] That much may be true. The issue in a case like this

---

[8] The "deliberate indifference" standard we adopt for § 1983 "failure to train" claims does not turn on the degree of fault (if any) that a plaintiff must show to make out an underlying claim of a constitution violation. For example, this Court has never determined what degree of culpability must be shown before the particular constitutional deprivation asserted in this case–a denial of due process right to medical care while in detention–is established. Indeed, in *Revere* v. *Massachusetts General Hospital*, 463 U. S. 239, 243–245 (1983), we reserved discussion of whether something less than Eighth Amendment's "deliberate indifference" test may be applicable in claims by detainees asserting violations of their due process right to medical care while in custody.

We need not resolve here the question in *Revere* for two reasons. First, petitioner has conceded that, as the the case comes to us, we must assume respondent's constitutional right to receive medical care was denied by city employees–whatever the nature of that right might be. See Tr. of Oral Arg. 8–9. Second, the proper standard for determining when a municipality will be liable under § 1983 for constitutional wrongs does not turn on any underlying culpability tests that determine when such wrongs have occurred. Cf. Brief for Respondent 27.

[9] The plurality opinion in *Tuttle* explained why this must be so:

"Obviously, if one retreats far enough from a constitutional violation some municipal 'policy' can be identified behind almost any...harm inflicted by a municipal official; for example, [a police officer] would never have killed Tuttle if Oklahoma City did not have a 'policy' of establishing a police force. But *Monell* must be taken to require proof of a city policy different in kind from this latter example before a claim can be sent to a jury on the theory that a particular violation was 'caused' by the municipal 'policy.'" *Tuttle*, 471 U. S., at 823.

Cf. also *Id.*, at 833, n. 9 (opinion of Brennan, J.).

one, however, is whether that training program is adequate; and if it is not, the question becomes whether such inadequate training can justifiably be said to represent "city policy." It may seem contrary to common sense to assert that a municipality will actually have a policy of not taking reasonable steps to train its employees. But it may happen that in light of the duties assigned to specific officers or employees the need for more or different training is so obvious, and the inadequacy so likely to result in the violation of constitutional rights, that the policymakers of the city can reasonably be said to have been deliberately indifferent to the need.[10] In that event, the failure to provide proper training may fairly be said to represent a policy for which the city is responsible, and for which the city may be held liable if it actually causes injury.[11]

In resolving the issue of a city's liability, the focus must be on adequacy of the training program in relation to the tasks the particular officers must perform. That a particular officer may be unsatisfactorily trained will not alone suffice to fasten liability on the city, for the officer's shortcomings may have resulted from factors other than a faulty training program. See *Springfield* v. *Kibbe*, 480 U. S. at 268 (O'CONNOR, J., dissenting); *Oklahoma City* v. *Tuttle, supra*, at 821 (opinion of REHNQUIST, J.). It may be, for example, that an otherwise sound program has occasionally been negligently administered. Neither will it suffice to prove that an injury or accident could have been avoided if an officer had had better or more training, sufficient to equip him to avoid the particular injury-causing conduct. Such a claim could be made about almost any encounter resulting in injury, yet not condemn the adequacy of the program to enable officers to respond properly to the usual and recurring situations with which they must deal. And plainly, adequately trained officers occasionally

[10] For example, city policy makers know to a moral certainty that their police officers will be required to arrest fleeing felons. The city has armed its officers with firearms, in part to allow them to complete this task. Thus, the need to train its officers in the constitutional limitations on the use of deadly force, see *Tennessee* v. *Garner*, 471 U. S. 1 (1985), can be said to be "so obvious," that failure to do so could properly be characterized as "deliberate indifference" to constitutional rights.

It could also be that the police, in exercising their discretion, so often violate constitutional rights that the need for further training must have been plainly obvious to the city policy makers, who, nevertheless, are "deliberately indifferent" to the need.

[11] The record indicates that city did train its officers and that training included first-aid instruction. See App. to Pet. for Cert. 4a. Petitioner argues that it could not have been obvious to the city that such training was insufficient to administer the written policy, which was itself constitutional. This is a question to be resolved on remand. See Part VI, *infra*.

make mistakes; the fact that they do says little about the training program or the legal basis for holding the city liable.

Moreover, for liability to attach in this circumstance the identified deficiency in a city's training program must be closely related to the ultimate injury. Thus in the case at hand, respondent must still prove that the deficiency in training actually caused the police officers' indifference to her medical needs.[12] Would the injury have been avoided had the employee been trained under a program that was not deficient in the identified respect? Predicting how a hypothetically well-trained officer would have acted under the circumstances may not be an easy task for the factfinder. particularly since matters of judgement may be involved, and since officers who are well trained are not free from error and perhaps might react very much like the untrained officer in similar circumstances. But judge and jury, doing their respective jobs, will be adequate to the task.

To adopt lesser standards of fault and causation would open municipalities to unprecedented liability under § 1983. In virtually every instance where a person has had his or her constitutional rights violated by a city employee, a 1983 plaintiff will be able to point to something the city "could have done" to prevent the unfortunate incident. See *Oklahoma City* v. *Tuttle, supra*, at 823 (opinion of REHNQUIST, J.). Thus, permitting cases against cities for their "failure to train" employees to go forward under § 1983 on a lesser standard of fault would result in *de facto respondeat superior* liability on municipalities–a result we rejected in *Monell*, 436 U. S., at 693–694. It would also engage the federal courts in an endless exercise of second-guessing municipal employee-training programs. This is an exercise we believe the federal courts are ill-suited to undertake, as well as one that would implicate serious questions of federalism. Cf. *Rizzo* v. *Goode*, 423 U. S. 362, 378–380 (1976).

Consequently, while claims such as respondent's–alleging that the city's failure to provide training to municipal employees resulted in the constitutional deprivation she suffered–are cognizable under § 1983, they can only yield liability against a municipality where that city's failure to train reflects deliberate indifference to the constitutional rights of its inhabitants.

---

[12] Respondent conceded as much at argument. See Tr. of Oral Arg. 50–51; cf. also *Oklahoma City* v. *Tuttle, supra,* at 831 (opinion of BREENAN, J.).

IV

The final question here is whether this case should be remanded for a new trial, or whether, as petitioner suggests, we should conclude that there are no possible grounds on which respondent can prevail. See Tr. of Oral Arg. 57–58. It is true that the evidence in the record now does not meet the standard of ¶ 1983 liability we have set forth above. But, the standard of proof the District Court ultimately imposed on respondent (which was consistent with Sixth Circuit precedent) was a lesser one than the one we adopt today, see Tr. 4–389–390. Whether respondent should have an opportunity to prove her case under the "deliberate indifference" rule we have adopted is a matter for the Court of Appeals to deal with on remand.

V

Consequently, for the reasons given above, we vacate the judgment of the Court of Appeals and remand this case for further proceedings consistent with this opinion.

It is so ordered

SUPREME COURT OF THE UNITED STATES

No. 86–1088

CITY OF CANTON, OHIO, PETITIONER *v.* GERALDINE HARRIS ET AL.

ON WRIT OF CERTIORARI TO THE UNITED STATES COURT OF APPEALS FOR THE SIXTH CIRCUIT

[FEBRUARY 28, 1989]

JUSTICE BRENNAN, concurring.

The Court's opinion, which I join, makes clear that the Court of Appeals is free to remand this case for a new trial.

SUPREME COURT OF THE UNITED STATES

No. 86–1088

CITY OF CANTON, OHIO, PETITIONER *v.* GERALDINE HARRIS ET AL.

ON WRIT OF CERTIORARI TO THE UNITED STATES COURT OF APPEALS FOR THE SIXTH CIRCUIT

[FEBRUARY 28, 1989]

JUSTICE O'CONNOR, with whom JUSTICE SCALIA and JUSTICE KENNEDY join, concurring in part and dissenting in part.

I join Parts I, II, and all of Part III of the Court's opinion except footnote 11, see *ante*, at n. 11. I thus agree that where municipal policymakers are confronted with an obvious need to train city personnel to avoid the violation of constitutional rights and they are deliberately indifferent to that need, the lack of necessary training may be appropriately considered a city "policy" subjecting the city itself to liability under our decision in *Monell* v. *New York City Dept. of Social Services*, 436 U. S. 658 (1978). As the Court observes, "[o]nly where a failure to train reflects a 'deliberate' or conscious' choice by a municipality–a 'policy' as defined by our prior cases–can a city be liable for such a failure under § 1983. *Ante*, at 10. I further agree that a § 1983 plaintiff pressing a "failure to train" claim must prove that the lack of training was the "cause" of the constitutional injury at issue and that this entails more than simply showing "but for" causation. *Ante*, at 11–12. Lesser requirements of fault and causation in this context would "open municipalities to unprecedented liability under § 1983," *ante*, at 12, and would pose serious federalism concerns. *Ante*, at 13.

My single point of disagreement with the majority is thus a small one. Because I believe, as the majority strongly hints, see *ibid*, that respondent has not and could not satisfy the fault and causation requirements we adopt today, I think it necessary to remand this case to the Court of Appeals for further proceedings. This case comes to us after a full trial during which respondent vigorously pursued numerous theories of municipal liability including an allegation that the city had a "custom" of not providing medical care to detainees suffering from emotional illnesses. Respondent thus had every opportunity and incentive to adduce the type of proof necessary to satisfy the deliberate indifference standard we adopt today. Rather than remand in this context, I would apply the deliberate indifference standard to the facts of this case. After undertaking that analysis below, I conclude that there is no evidence in the record indicating that the city of Canton has been deliberately indifferent to the constitutional rights of pretrial detainees.

I

In *Monell*, the Court held that municipal liability can be imposed under § 1983 only where the municipality, as an entity, can be said to be "responsible" for a constitutional violation committed by one of its employees. "[T]he touchstone of the § 1983 action against a government body is an allegation that official policy is responsible for a deprivation of rights protected by the Constitution." 436 U. S., at 690. The Court found that the language of § 1983, and rejection of the "Sherman Amendment" by the 42nd Congress, were both strong indicators that the framers of the Civil Rights Act of 1871 did not intend that municipal governments be held vicariously liable for the constitutional torts of their employees. Thus § 1983 plaintiff seeking to attach liability to the city for acts of one of its employees may not rest on the employment relationship alone, both fault and causation *as to the acts or omissions of the city itself* must be proved. The Court reaffirms these requirements today.

Where, as here, a claim of municipal liability is predicated upon a failure to act, the requisite degree of fault must be shown by proof of a background of events and circumstances which establish that the "policy of inaction" is the functional equivalent of a decision by the city itself to violate the Constitution. Without some form of notice to the city, and the opportunity to conform to constitutional dictates both what it does and what it chooses not to do, the failure to train theory of liability could completely engulf *Monell*, imposing liability without regard to fault. Moreover, absent a requirement that the lack of training at issue bear a very close causal connection to the violation of constitutional rights, the failure to train theory of municipal liability could impose "prophylactic" duties on municipal governments only remotely connected to underlying constitutional requirements themselves.

Such results would be directly contrary to the intent of the drafters of § 1983. The central vice of the Sherman Amendment, as noted by the Court's opinion in *Monell*, was that it "impose[d] a species of vicarious liability on municipalities since it could be construed to impose liability even if the municipality *did not know* of an impending or ensuing riot or did not have the wherewithal to do anything about it." 436 U. S., at 692, n. 57 (emphasis added). Moreover, as noted in *Monell*, the authors of § 1 of the Ku Klux Klan Act did not intend to create any new rights or duties beyond those contained in the Constitution. *Id.*, at 684–685. Thus, § 1 was referred to as "reenacting the Constitution." Cong. Globe, 42 Cong., 1st Sess., 569 (1871) (Rep. Edmunds). Representative Bingham, the author of § 1 of the Fourteenth Amendment, saw the purpose of § 1983 as "the enforcement...of the Constitution on behalf of every individual citizen of the Republic...to extent of the rights guaranteed to him by the Constitution." Id., at App. 81. See also *Chapman* v. *Houston Welfare Rights Organization*, 441 U. S. 600, 617 (1979) ("[Section] 1 of the Civil Rights Act of 1871 did not provide for any substantive rights–equal or otherwise. As introduced and enacted, it served only to insure that an individual had a cause of action for violations of the Constitution"). Thus § 1983 is not a "federal good government act" for municipalities. Rather it creates a federal cause of action against persons, including municipalities, who deprive citizens of the United States of their constitutional rights.

Sensitive to these concerns, the Court's opinion correctly requires a high degree of fault on the part of city officials before an omission that is not in itself unconstitutional can support liability as a municipal policy under *Monell*. As the Court indicates, "it may happen that...the need for more or different training is so obvious, and the inadequacy so likely to result in the violation of constitutional rights, that the policymakers of the city can reasonably be said to have been deliberately indifferent to the need." *Ante*, at 10–11. Where a § 1983 plaintiff can establish that the facts available to city policymakers put them on actual or constructive notice that the particular omission is substantially certain to result in the violation of the constitutional rights of their citizens, the dictates of *Monell* are satisfied. Only then can it be said that the municipality has made " 'a deliberate choice to follow a course of action...from among various alternatives.' " *Ante*, at 10, quoting *Pembaur* v. *Cincinnati*, 475 U. S. 469, 483–484 (1986).

In my view, it could be shown that the need for training was obvious in one of two ways. First, a municipality could fail to train its employees concerning a clear constitutional duty implicated in recurrent situations that a particular employee is certain to face. As the majority notes, see *ante*, at 11, n. 10, the constitutional limitations established by this Court on the use of deadly force by police officers present one such situation. The constitutional duty of the individual officer is clear, and it is equally clear that failure to inform city personnel of that duty will create an extremely high risk that constitutional violations will ensue.

The claim in this case–that police officers inadequately trained in diagnosing the symptoms of emotional illness–falls far short of the kind of "obvious" need for training that would support a finding of deliberate indifference to constitutional rights on the part of the city. As the Court's opinion observes, *ante,* at 9, n. 8, this Court has not yet addressed the precise nature of the obligations that the Due Process Clause places upon the police to seek medical care for pretrial detainees who have been *physically* injured while being apprehended by the police. See *Revere* v. *Massachusetts General Hospital*, 463 U. S. 239, 246 (1983) (Rehnquist, J., concurring). There are thus no clear constitutional guideposts for municipalities in this area, and the diagnosis of mental illness is not one of the "usual and recurring situations with which [the police] must deal." Ante, at 11–12. The lack of training at issue here is not the kind of omission that can be characterized, in and of itself, as a "deliberate indifference" to constitutional rights.

Second, I think municipal liability for failure to train may be proper where it can be shown that policymakers were aware of, and acquiesced in, a pattern of constitutional violations involving the exercise of police discretion. In such cases, the need for training may not be obvious from the outset, but a pattern of constitution violations could put the municipality on notice that its officers confront the particular situation on a regular basis, and that they often react in a manner contrary to constitutional requirements. The lower courts that have applied the "deliberate indifference" standard we adopt today have required a showing of a pattern of violations from which a kind of "tacit authorization" by city policymakers can be inferred. See, *e.g., Fiacco* v. *City of Rensselaer,* 783 F. 2d 319, 327 (CA2 1986) (multiple incidents required for finding of deliberate indifference); *Patzner* v. *Burkett,* 779 F. 2d 1363, 1367 (CA8 1985) ("[A] municipality may be liable if it had notice of prior misbehavior by its officers and failed to take remedial steps amounting to deliberate indifference to the offensive acts"); *Languirand* v. *Hayden,* 747 F. 2d 220, 227–228 (CA5 1983) (municipal liability for failure to train requires "evidence at least of a pattern of similar incidents in which citizens were injured or endangered"); *Wellington* v. *Daniels,* 717 F. 2d 932, 936 (CA4 1983) ("[A] failure to supervise gives rise to § 1983 liability, however, only in those situations where there is a history of widespread abuse. Only then may knowledge be imputed to the supervisory personnel").

The Court's opinion recognizes this requirement, see *ante,* at 11, and n. 10, but declines to evaluate the evidence presented in this case in light of the new legal standard. *Ante,* at 13. From the outset of this litigation, respondent has pressed a claim that the city of Canton had a custom of denying medical care to pretrial detainees with emotional disorders. See Amended Complaint ¶28, App. 27. Indeed, up to and including oral argument before this Court, counsel for respondent continued to assert that respondent was attempting to hinge municipal liability upon "both a custom of denying medical care to a certain class of prisoners, and a failure to train police that led to this particular violation." Tr. of Oral Arg. 37–38. At the time respondent filed her complaint in 1980, it was clear that proof of the existence of a custom entailed a showing of "practices...so permanent and well settled as to constitute a 'custom or usage' with the force of law." *Adickes* v. *S. H. Kress & Co.,* 398 U. S. 144, 168 (1970); see also *Garner* v. *Memphis Police Department,* 600 F. 2d 52, 54–55, and n. 4 (CA6 1979) (discussing proof of custom in light of *Monell*).

Whatever the prevailing standard at the time concerning liability for failure to train, respondent thus had every incentive to adduce proof at trial of a pattern of violations to support her claim that the city had an unwritten custom of denying medical care to emotionally ill detainees. In fact, respondent presented no testimony from any witness indicating that there had been past incidents of "deliberate indifference" to the medical needs of emotionally disturbed detainees or that any other circumstance had put the city on actual or constructive notice of a need for additional training in this regard. At trial, David Maser, who was Chief of Police of the city of Canton from 1971 to 1980, testified without contradiction that during his tenure he received no complaints that detainees in the Canton jails were not being accorded proper medical treatment. 4 Tr. 347–348. Former Officer Cherry, who had served as a jailer for the Canton Police Department, indicated that he had never had to seek medical treatment for persons who were emotionally upset at the prospect of arrest, because they usually calmed down when a member of the department spoke with them or one of the family members arrived. *Id.*, at 83–84. There is quite simply nothing in this record to indicate that the city of Canton had any reason to suspect that failing to provide this kind of training would lead to injuries of any kind, let alone violations of the Due Process Clause. None of the Courts of Appeal that already apply the standard we adopt today would allow respondent to take her claim to a jury based on the facts she adduced at trial. See *Patzner* v. *Burkett*, 779 F. 2d, at 1367 (summary judgment proper under "deliberate indifference" standard where evidence of only single incident adduced); *Languirand* v. *Hayden*, 717 F. 2d, at 229 (reversing jury verdict rendered under failure to train theory where there was no evidence of prior incidents to support a finding that municipal policymakers were "consciously indifferent" to constitutional rights); *Wellington* v. *Daniels*, 717 F. 2d, at 937 (affirming judgment n.o.v. for municipality under "deliberate indifference" standard where evidence of only a single incident was presented at trial); compare *Fiacco* v. *City of Rensselaer*, 783 F. 2d, at 328–332 (finding evidence of "deliberate indifference" sufficient to support jury verdict where a pattern of similar violations was shown at trial).

Allowing an inadequate training claim such as this one to go to the jury based upon a single incident would only invite jury nullification of *Monell*. "To infer the existence of a city policy from the isolated misconduct of a single, low-level officer, and then to hold the city liable on the basis of that policy,would amount to permitting precisely the theory of strict respondeat superior liability rejected in *Monell.*" *Oklahoma City* v. *Tuttle*, 471 U. S. 808, 831 (1985) (BRENNAN, J., concurring). As the authors of the Ku Klux Klan Act themselves realized, the resources of local government are not inexhaustible. The grave step of shifting of those resources to particular areas where constitutional violations are likely to result through the deterrent power of § 1983 should certainly not be taken on the basis of an isolated incident. If § 1983 and the Constitution require the city of Canton to provide detailed medical care and psychological training to its police officers, or to station paramedics at its jails, other city services will necessarily suffer, including those with far more direct implications for the protection of constitutional rights. Because respondent's evidence falls short of establishing the high degree of fault on the part of the city required by our decision today, and because there is no indication that respondent could produce any new proof in this regard, I would reverse the judgment of the Court of Appeals and order entry of judgment for the city.

Appendix C

102D CONGRESS
2D SESSION

H. R. 4429

To amend title I of the Omnibus Crime Control and Safe Streets Act of 1968 to increase national awareness concerning high speed motor vehicle pursuits involving law enforcement officers and the individuals pursued, and for other purposes.

IN THE HOUSE OF REPRESENTATIVES

MARCH 11, 1992

Mr. Dorgan of North Dakota introduced the following bill; which was referred to the Committee on the Judiciary

---

A BILL

To amend title I of the Omnibus Crime Control and Safe Streets Act of 1968 to increase national awareness concerning high speed motor vehicle pursuits involving law enforcement officers and the individuals pursued, and for other purposes.

Be it enacted by the Senate and House of Representatives of the United States of America in Congress assembled,

SECTION 1. SHORT TITLE.

This Act may be cited as the "National Pursuit Awareness Act of 1992".

SEC. 2. FINDINGS.

Congress finds that–

(1) accidents occurring as a result of high speed motor vehicle pursuits caused by drug offenders and other motorists fleeing from law enforcement officers are becoming increasingly common across the United States;

(2) the extent of this problem makes it essential for all law enforcement agencies to develop and implement both policies and training procedures for dealing with these pursuits;

(3) to demonstrate leadership in response to this national problem, all Federal law enforcement agencies should develop and coordinate policies and procedures governing pursuits, and provide assistance to State and local law enforcement agencies in instituting such policies and training; and

(4) such policies should balance the need for prompt apprehension of dangerous criminals with the threat to the safety of the general public, and should specifically define, at a minimum, what constitutes a pursuit, the requirements necessary to initiate a pursuit, and regulations to continue or terminate a pursuit.

SEC. 3. NATIONAL PROGRAM ON MOTOR VEHICLE PURSUITS BY LAW ENFORCEMENT OFFICERS.

(a) MOTOR VEHICLE PURSUITS.–Section 501(b) of title I of the Omnibus Crime Control and Safe Streets Act of 1968 is amended–

(1) by striking the period at the end of paragraph (21) and adding "; and"; and

(2) by adding at the end the following:

"(22) programs that increase awareness and improve public safety through implementation of policies and training procedures to regulate the use of vehicular pursuit by law enforcement officers of criminal suspects.".

(b) FORMULA GRANT REDUCTION FOR NONCOMPLIANCE.–Section 506 of title I of the Omnibus Crime Control and Safe Streets Act of 1968 is amended by adding at the end the following:

"(g) In order not to reduced the funds available under this subpart by 25 percent (for redistribution to other participating States), a State shall, on the first day of each fiscal year succeeding the first fiscal year beginning after September 30, 1994, meet the following requirements:

"(1) Have in effect throughout the State in such fiscal year a law which–

"(A) makes it unlawful for the driver of a motor vehicle to increase speed or take any other evasive action if a law enforcement officer signals the driver to stop the motor vehicle; and

"(B) provides a minimum penalty of 3 months imprisonment, and seizure of the violator's vehicle, for a violation of the offense described in subparagraph (A).

"(2) Require each public agency in the State which employs law enforcement officers who in the course of employment may conduct a motor vehicle pursuit–

"(A) to have in effect in such fiscal year a policy which describes the manner in which, and the circumstances in which, such a pursuit should be conducted and terminated;

"(B) to train all law enforcement officers of the agency in accordance with such policy;

"(C) to transmit to the State in such fiscal year a report containing information on each motor vehicle pursuit conducted by a law enforcement officer of the agency.".

SEC. 4. REPORTING REQUIREMENT.

Not later than 180 days after the date of the enactment of this Act, the Attorney General, the Secretary of Agriculture, the Secretary of the Interior, the Secretary of the Treasury, the Chief of the Capitol Police, and the

Administrator of the General Services Administration shall each transmit to Congress a report containing–

(1) the policy of the respective department or agency on motor vehicle pursuits by law enforcement officers of the department or agency; and

(2) a description of procedures being used to train law enforcement officers of the department or agency in implementation of such policy.

The policy of a department or agency contained in a report required by this section shall meet the requirements of section 506(g) of title I of the Omnibus Crime Control and Safe Streets Act of 1968, as added by section 3(b) of this Act.

Appendix D

VEHICULAR PURSUIT MODEL POLICY

	Effective Date **December 1, 1989**	*Number*
Subject **Vehicular Pursuit**		
Reference		*Special Instructions*
Distribution	*Revelation Date* **November 30, 1990**	*No. Pages*

I. PURPOSE

The purpose of this policy is to state the guidelines to be followed during vehicular pursuit.

II. POLICY

Vehicular pursuit of fleeing suspects presents a danger to the lives of the public, officers and suspects involved in the pursuit. It is the policy of this department to protect all persons' lives to the extent possible when enforcing the law. In addition, it is the responsibility of the department to assist officers in the safe performance of their duties. To effect these obligations, it shall be the policy of the department to narrowly regulate the manner in which vehicular pursuit is undertaken and performed.

III. DEFINITION

A. Vehicular Pursuit: An active attempt by an officer in an authorized emergency vehicle to apprehend fleeing suspects who are attempting to avoid apprehension through evasive tactics.

IV. PROCEDURES

A. Initiation of Pursuit

1. The decision to initiate pursuit must be used on the pursuing officer's conclusion that the immediate danger to the public created by the pursuit is less than the immediate or potential danger to the public should the suspect remain at large.
2. Any law enforcement officer in an authorized emergency vehicle may initiate a vehicular pursuit when ALL of the following criteria are met:
   a. The suspect exhibits the intention to avoid arrest by using a vehicle to flee apprehension for an alleged felony of misdemeanor that would normally require a full custody arrest;
   b. The suspect operating the vehicle refuses to stop at the direction of the officer, and

c. The suspect, if allowed to flee, would present a danger to human life or cause serious injury.

3. The pursuing officer shall consider the following factors in determining whether to initiate pursuit:
   a. The performance capabilities of the pursuit vehicle;
   b. The condition of the road surface upon which the pursuit is being conducted;
   c. The amount of vehicular and pedestrian traffic in the area; and
   d. Weather conditions.

B. Pursuit Officer Responsibilities

1. The pursuing officer shall immediately notify communications center personnel that a pursuit is under way. The officer shall provide communications personnel with the following information:
   a. Unit identification;
   b. Location, speed and direction of travel of the fleeing vehicle;
   c. Description and license plate number, if known, of the fleeing vehicle;
   d. Number of occupants in the fleeing vehicle, and descriptions, where possible; and
   e. Reasons supporting the decision to pursue.
2. Failure to provide this information to communications personnel may result in an immediate decision by a field supervisor assigned to monitor the pursuit to order its termination.
3. The primary unit shall reduce the level of pursuit to that of support or backup unit where:
   a. The fleeing vehicle comes under the surveillance of an air unit; or
   b. Another vehicle has been assigned primary pursuit responsibility.
4. Any primary or backup unit sustaining damage to, or failure of essential vehicular equipment during pursuit shall not be permitted to continue in the pursuit. The unit shall notify communications so that another unit may be assigned to the pursuit.

C. Communications Center Responsibilities

1. Upon notification that a pursuit is in progress, communications personnel shall immediately advise a field supervisor of essential information regarding the pursuit.
2. Communications personnel shall carry out the following activities and responsibilities during the pursuit:
   a. Receive and record all incoming information on the pursuit and the pursued vehicle;
   b. Control all radio communications and clear the radio channels of all nonemergency calls;
   c. Obtain criminal record and vehicle checks of the suspects;
   d. Coordinate and dispatch backup assistance and air support units under the direction of the field supervisor; and
   e. Notify neighboring jurisdictions, where practical, when pursuit may extend into their locality.

D. Field Supervisors Responsibilities During Vehicular Pursuit

1. Upon notification that a vehicular pursuit incident is in progress, the field supervisor shall assume responsibility for the monitoring and control of the pursuit as it progresses.
2. The field supervisor shall continuously review the incoming data to determine

whether the pursuit should be continued or terminated.

3. In controlling the pursuit incident, the field supervisor shall be responsible for coordination of the pursuit as follows:
   a. Directing pursuit vehicles or air support units into or out of the pursuit;
   b. Redesignation of primary, support or other backup vehicle responsibilities;
   c. Approval or disapproval, and coordination of pursuit tactics; and
   d. Approval or disapproval to leave jurisdiction to continue pursuit.
4. The field supervisor may approve and assign additional backup vehicles or air support units to assist the primary and backup pursuit vehicles based on an analysis of:
   a. The nature of the offense for which the pursuit was initiated;
   b. The number of suspects and the any known propensity for violence;
   c. The number of officers in the pursuit vehicles;
   d. Any damage or injuries to the assigned primary and backup vehicle or officers;
   e. The number of officers necessary to make an arrest at the conclusion of the pursuit; and
   f. Any other clear and articulable facts that would warrant the increased hazards caused by numerous pursuit vehicles.

E. Traffic Regulations During Pursuit
1. Each unit authorized to engage in vehicular pursuit shall be required to activate headlights and all emergency vehicle equipment prior to beginning pursuit.
2. Officers engaged in pursuit shall at all times drive in a manner exercising reasonable care for the safety of themselves and all other persons and property within the pursuit area.
3. Officers are permitted to suspend conformance with normal traffic regulations during pursuit as long as reasonable care is used when driving in a manner not otherwise permitted, and the maneuver is reasonably necessary to gain control of the suspect.

F. Pursuit Tactics
1. Unless expressly authorized by a field supervisor, pursuit shall be limited to the assigned primary and backup vehicles. Officers are not otherwise permitted to join the pursuit team, or follow the pursuit on parallel streets.
2. Officers may not intentionally use their vehicle to bump or ram the suspect's vehicle in order to force the vehicle to a stop off the road or in a ditch.
3. Departmental policy pertaining to use of deadly force shall be adhered to during the pursuit.

G. Termination of Pursuit
1. A decision to terminate pursuit may be the most rational means of preserving the lives and property of both the public, and the officers and suspects engaged in pursuit. Pursuit may be terminated by the pursuing officer, the field supervisor or chief executive officer of the department.
2. Pursuit shall be immediately terminated in any of the following circumstances:
   a. Weather or traffic conditions substantially increase the danger of pursuit beyond the worth of apprehending the suspect;
   b. The distance between the pursuit and fleeing vehicles is so great that further pursuit is futile; or
   c. The danger posed by continued pursuit to the public, the officers or the

suspects is greater than the value of apprehending the suspect(s).

3. The pursuing officer shall relay this information to communications personnel, along with any further information acquired which may assist in an arrest at a later date.

H. Interjurisdictional Pursuits

1. The pursuing officer shall notify communications when it is likely that a pursuit will continue into a neighboring jurisdiction, or across the state line.
2. Pursuit into a bordering state shall conform with the department's inter-jurisdictional pursuit agreement and state law.

I. The field supervisor shall prepare a comprehensive analysis of the pursuit, and forward it to the chief executive officer of the agency.

BY ORDER OF

____

CHIEF OF POLICE

This model policy is intended to serve as a guide for the police executive who is interested in formulating a written procedure to govern vehicular pursuit. The police executive is advised to refer to all federal, state and municipal statutes ordinances, regulations, and judicial and administrative decisions to ensure that the policy he or she seeks to implement meets the unique needs of the jurisdiction.

INDEX

R